Where the Girls Are: The Facts About Gender Equity in Education

Christianne Corbett
Catherine Hill, Ph.D.
Andresse St. Rose

Published by AAUW
1111 Sixteenth St. N.W.
Washington, DC 20036
Phone: 202/728-7602
Fax: 202/463-7169
TDD: 202/785-7777
E-mail: helpline@aauw.org
Web: www.aauw.org

First printing: May 2008

Library of Congress Control Number: 2008920525
ISBN: 978-1-879922-38-9

023-08 4M 5/08

This report was made possible by generous contributions to the AAUW Educational Foundation by

Lilo and Gerard Leeds

and

The Mooneen Lecce Giving Circle

The giving circle honors the legacy of Mooneen Lecce, whose passion for the mission of AAUW continues to inspire volunteerism and charitable giving dedicated to improving the lives of women and girls.

Table of Contents

Figures

Chapter 2

Chapter 3

Chapter 4

Appendix A. NAEP Supplementary Figures

Appendix B. SAT and ACT Supplementary Figures

Foreword

Women and girls have made remarkable gains in education during the past 100 years, disrupting the belief—now largely unspoken—that boys and men are better "suited" to intellectual work. Today, few journalists or policy-makers would publicly admit to such a prejudice. As former Harvard University president Lawrence Summers recently discovered, too many female scholars hold the "right" degrees and professional credentials to allow a public reference to male superiority in any field to stand unchallenged.

Since 1881, the American Association of University Women has helped make this progress possible. AAUW released its landmark study, *The AAUW Report: How Schools Shortchange Girls*, in 1992, sparking a national debate on gender equity in education. Building on the success of that report, AAUW developed a multiyear research agenda on gender equity in education. Research reports released since 1992 have focused on school climate and sexual harassment, girls in science and technology, race and gender on campus, and other topics. This substantial body of research established AAUW as a leader on the issue of educational equity.

It is a testament to the success of the efforts by AAUW and others that the gender equity debate has taken a new twist in which boys are cast as the disadvantaged gender. *Where the Girls Are: The Facts About Gender Equity in Education* makes clear that girls' gains have not come at the expense of boys. In addition, the report goes beyond gender to look at other factors that influence student achievement—specifically family income level and race/ethnicity—and finds that many girls as well as boys are not acquiring the educational skills needed to succeed in the 21st-century economy. This report illustrates that while educational trends for both girls and boys are generally positive, disparities by race/ethnicity and family income level exist and are critical to understanding the landscape of education in America today.

Barbara L O'Connor

Barbara O'Connor, President
AAUW Educational Foundation

Acknowledgments

AAUW thanks Elizabeth Woody for a concept paper that inspired this research. AAUW is grateful for the guidance of members of its Research Advisory Council: Sousan Arafeh, Joanne Cohoon, Sumru Erkut, Lynn Fountain, Gloria Thomas, Anne Valk, and Verna Williams. AAUW also acknowledges the exceptional work of editor Susan K. Dyer and cover designer Alan B. Callander. Finally, AAUW thanks the following staff members for contributing to this project: Linda Hallman and Jill Birdwhistell, AAUW Executive Office; Lisa Maatz and Lauren Kennedy, AAUW Public Policy and Government Relations Department; and Laura Stepp and Carol Rognrud, AAUW Development Department.

About the Authors

Christianne Corbett is a research associate at AAUW. She has a master's degree in cultural anthropology from the University of Colorado and bachelor's degrees in government and aerospace engineering from the University of Notre Dame.

Catherine Hill is director of research at AAUW, where she focuses on higher education and women's economic security. She has a bachelor's and a master's degree from Cornell University and a doctorate in public policy from Rutgers University.

Andresse St. Rose is a graduate research assistant at AAUW and a doctoral candidate in education policy at George Washington University. She has a bachelor's degree in biology from Hamilton College and a master's degree in higher education administration from Boston College.

Executive Summary

Where the Girls Are: The Facts About Gender Equity in Education presents a comprehensive look at girls' educational achievement during the past 35 years, paying special attention to the relationship between girls' and boys' progress. Analyses of results from national standardized tests such as the National Assessment of Educational Progress (NAEP) and the SAT and ACT college entrance examinations, as well as other measures of educational achievement, provide an overall picture of trends in gender equity from elementary school to college and beyond. Differences among girls and among boys by race/ethnicity and family income level are evaluated. Together these analyses support three overarching facts about gender equity in schools today:

1. Girls' successes don't come at boys' expense.

Educational achievement is not a zero-sum game, in which a gain for one group results in a corresponding loss for the other. If girls' success comes at the expense of boys, one would expect to see boys' scores decline as girls' scores rise, but this has not been the case. Geographical patterns further demonstrate the positive connection between girls' and boys' educational achievement. In states where girls do well on tests, boys also do well, and states with low test scores among boys tend to also have low scores among girls.

High school and college graduation rates present a similar story. Women are attending and graduating from high school and college at a higher rate than are their male peers, but these gains have not come at men's expense. Indeed, the proportion of young men graduating from high school and earning college degrees today is at an all-time high. Women have made more rapid gains in earning college degrees, especially among older students, where women outnumber men by a ratio of almost 2-to-1. The gender gap in college attendance is almost absent among those entering college directly after graduating from high school, however, and both women and men are more likely to graduate from college today than ever before.

2. On average, girls' and boys' educational performance has improved.

From standardized tests in elementary and secondary school to college entrance examinations, average test scores have risen or remained stable for both girls and boys in recent decades. Similarly, both women and men are more likely to graduate from high school and college today than ever before.

3. Understanding disparities by race/ethnicity and family income level is critical to understanding girls' and boys' achievement.

Family income level and race/ethnicity are closely associated with academic performance. On standardized tests such as the NAEP, SAT, and ACT, children from the lowest-income families have the lowest average test scores, with an incremental rise in family income associated with a rise in test scores. Race/ethnicity is also strongly connected to test scores, with African American and Hispanic children—both girls and boys—scoring lower than white and Asian American children score.

Gender differences in educational achievement vary by race/ethnicity and family income level. For example, girls often have outperformed boys within each racial/ethnic group on the NAEP reading test. When broken down by race/ethnicity, however, this gender gap is found to be most consistent among white students, less so among African American students, and least among Hispanic students. Similarly, boys overall have outperformed girls on both the math and verbal portions of the SAT. Disaggregated by family income level, however, the male advantage on the verbal portion of the SAT is consistently seen only among students from low-income families. Gender differences seen in one group are not always replicated within another group.

Drawing from educational indicators from fourth grade to college, this report examines gender equity trends since the 1970s. The results put to rest fears of a "boys' crisis" in education, demonstrating that girls' gains have not come at boys' expense. Overall, educational outcomes for both girls and boys have generally improved or stayed the same. Girls have made especially rapid gains in many areas, but boys are also gaining ground on most indicators of educational achievement. Large discrepancies by race/ethnicity and family income level remain. These long-standing inequalities could be considered a "crisis" in the sense that action is needed urgently. But the crisis is not specific to boys; rather, it is a crisis for African American, Hispanic, and low-income children.

Chapter 1

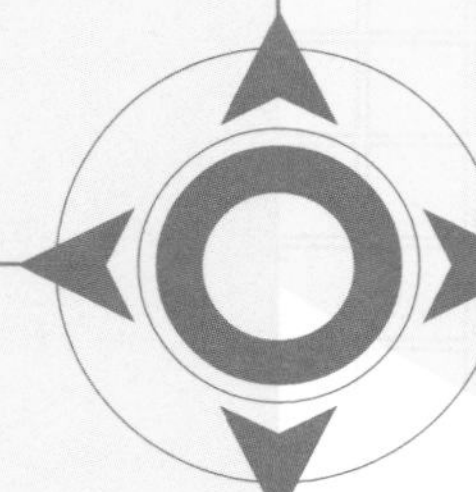

Where the Girls Are: Refuting the Boys' Crisis

Women and girls have made tremendous progress in education during the past 100 years. Throughout the first part of the 20th century, colleges could—and did—openly exclude or limit the number of female students. The passage of Title IX of the Education Amendments of 1972 marked the recognition by Congress that girls and boys hold the right to equal educational opportunities[1] and put an end to overt displays of gender bias. In the ensuing decades, women and girls have made progress at every level of education. Today, women make up a majority of undergraduates on college campuses. Women also have made rapid progress in some historically male fields, such as biology, chemistry, and mathematics, and are nearly as likely as men to pursue advanced degrees in medicine, law, and business.

Yet many people remain uncomfortable with the educational and professional advances of girls and women, especially when they threaten to outdistance their male peers. *The AAUW Report: How Schools Shortchange Girls*, published in 1992, set off a stormy public debate fueled, at least in part, by this discomfort. The report found that girls received less attention in the classroom than boys did and girls were not well represented in math-related fields. As the "girls' crisis" received increasing attention, critics countered that boys were the new disadvantaged group, facing discrimination in schools now designed to favor girls. From the incendiary book *The War Against Boys: How Misguided Feminism Is Harming Our Young Men* (Sommers, 2000) to more subtle insinuations such as the *New York Times* headline "At Colleges, Women Are Leaving Men in the Dust" (Lewin, 2006), a backlash against the achievements of girls and women emerged.

Building on work by Mead (2006), Susan S. Klein, et al. (2007), and others, *Where the Girls Are: The Facts About Gender Equity in Education* refutes the notion of a "boys' crisis" in education today. The report provides information on trends in educational achievement based on data from the National Assessment of Educational Progress (NAEP), college entrance examinations, and other educational indicators, such as high school and college graduation rates.

[1] Title IX states, "No person in the U.S. shall, on the basis of sex, be excluded from participation in, be denied the benefits of, or be subjected to discrimination under any education program or activity receiving Federal financial assistance."

Information on educational achievement is examined by gender, race/ethnicity, and family income level. Using both published and unpublished sources, the report presents a comprehensive picture of recent achievements by girls and boys in the U.S. educational system.

This chapter presents the case against the existence of a boys' crisis, drawing on data analyses presented in chapters 2, 3, and 4. Chapter 2 provides information on trends in NAEP test scores of elementary- and secondary-school girls and boys. Chapter 3 documents trends in test scores by gender for two college entrance examinations: the SAT I: Reasoning Exam (more commonly called the SAT) and the ACT. Chapter 4 uses data from the U.S. Census Bureau to explore other measures of educational achievement such as high school and college graduation rates and concludes with a discussion of the "payoff" of these credentials in terms of wages. Chapter 5 calls for a refocus of public attention from the "gender wars" to the longstanding divisions in the U.S. educational system by race/ethnicity and family income level.

Where the Girls Are considers gender differences in educational achievement with attention to race/ethnicity and family income level. Despite the vast literature on education, analysis of gender differences *within* racial/ethnic and income groups is surprisingly uncommon. For example, Lubienski's review of mathematics education research from 1982 to 1998 revealed that "only 3 of the 3,011 articles considered ethnicity, class and gender together" (2001, p. 3). Even the U.S. Department of Education's latest reports of the NAEP long-term trend assessment and other key indicators of educational achievement do not disaggregate scores by gender within family income levels or racial/ethnic groups (U.S. Department of Education, National Center for Education Statistics, 2004, 2005a). Standardized test scores and graduation rates are not the only measures of educational progress, but they are widely acknowledged to be valid measures of achievement.[2]

Taken together, these analyses support three overarching conclusions:

---

[2] In all chapters, differences between groups are presented in the text only if they are statistically significant (unlikely to occur by chance [$p<0.05$]).

1. Girls' successes don't come at boys' expense.

Girls' educational successes have not—and should not—come at the expense of boys. If girls' achievements come at the expense of boys, one would expect to see boys' scores decline as girls' scores rise, but boys' average test scores have improved alongside girls' scores in recent decades. For example, girls' average scores on the NAEP mathematics test have risen during the past three decades—as have boys' scores (indeed, older boys retain a small lead in math). Girls tend to earn higher average scores on the NAEP reading assessments, but this lead has narrowed or remained the same during the past three decades.

Geographical patterns further demonstrate the positive connection between girls' and boys' educational achievement. In states where girls do well on tests, boys also do well, and states with low average test scores among boys tend to have low scores among girls. For example, test scores on the 2007 main NAEP fourth-grade math assessment by state show that the five highest-scoring states for boys—Massachusetts, New Jersey, New Hampshire, Kansas, and Minnesota—were also the highest-scoring states for girls. Similarly, three of the four states with the lowest scores for boys—Mississippi, New Mexico, and Alabama—were also three of the lowest-scoring states for girls (U.S. Department of Education, National Center for Education Statistics, 2007g).

On both college entrance exams, boys retain a small, consistent lead. On the SAT, the largest gender gap occurs on the math exam in favor of boys. In contrast to the NAEP exam, boys maintain an advantage on the SAT verbal exam as well. Boys also have slightly higher average ACT composite scores. Boys perform better on the ACT mathematics and science sections, and girls perform better on the English and reading sections.

High school graduation rates and college attendance present a similar story. Women are attending and graduating from high school and college at a higher rate than are their male peers, but these gains have not come at men's expense. Indeed, the proportion of young men graduating from high school and earning college degrees today is at an all-time high. Women have made more rapid gains in earning college degrees, but both women and men are more likely to graduate from college today than ever before, and among traditional-age (under age 24) undergraduates from high-income families, men are still more likely than women to attend college.

Perhaps the most compelling evidence against the existence of a boys' crisis is that men continue to outearn women in the workplace. Among all women and men working full time, year round, women's median annual earnings were 77 percent of men's earnings in 2005 (Institute for Women's Policy Research, 2007). Looking at the college-educated, full-time work force one year out of college, women earned 80 percent of men's earnings on average in 2001, and 10 years out of college, women earned only 69 percent of men's earnings in 2003 (AAUW Educational Foundation, 2007). After controlling for factors known to affect earnings, regression analyses demonstrate that a portion of these pay gaps remains unexplained (ibid.).

2. On average, girls' and boys' educational performance has improved.

From standardized tests in elementary and secondary school to college entrance examinations, average test scores have risen or remained stable for both girls and boys in recent decades. This rise reflects gains among both low- and high-achieving students. A larger proportion of fourth and eighth graders in all racial/ethnic groups scored at or above a basic level on the main NAEP math and reading assessments in 2007 compared to 1992. Likewise, overall scores on college entrance examinations have risen since the mid-1990s for both girls and boys. Average ACT scores for both girls and boys rose between 1995 and 2007 in both English and math, and between 1994 and 2004, average SAT math and verbal scores also rose for both girls and boys. While the number of girls taking these exams has risen, so too has the number of boys. Girls taking the tests outnumber boys taking the tests, just as women outnumber men on college campuses. Yet the rising number of girls taking these exams has not deterred boys, and the number of boys taking the SAT and ACT is higher today than ever before.

On average, girls' and boys' performance in high school and college has also improved. Girls' and boys' grades in high school are higher today than in 1990, and despite a lack of consensus on the actual number of dropouts, researchers agree that overall graduation rates for boys have improved (Greene & Winters, 2005; Mishel & Roy, 2006). The number and percentage of both women and men attending and graduating from college are higher than ever before and continue to rise.

3. Understanding disparities by race/ethnicity and family income level is critical to understanding girls' and boys' achievement.

Family income level and race/ethnicity are closely associated with academic performance. On standardized tests such as the NAEP, SAT, and ACT, children from the lowest-income families have the lowest average test scores, with an incremental rise in family income associated with a rise in test scores. Race/ethnicity is also strongly associated with test scores, with African American and Hispanic children scoring lower on average than white and Asian American children. African American and Hispanic students and students from low-income families also have lower high school and college graduation rates than do Asian American and white students and students from higher-income families.

African American and Hispanic girls have a great deal in common with African American and Hispanic boys in terms of educational performance. For example, while average ACT English scores improved from 1995 to 2007 for Asian American and white girls and boys, scores for African American and Hispanic girls and boys either stayed the same or declined. As another example, the U.S. Census Bureau reported in 2006 that, overall, approximately 4 percent more women than men ages 25 to 29 had completed high school. But while 95 percent of white women had completed high school, only 67 percent of Hispanic women and 61 percent of Hispanic men had done so, resulting in a gap of 28 percentage points between white and Hispanic women and a much smaller gap of 6 percentage points between Hispanic women and men.

Gender differences in educational achievement vary by race/ethnicity and family income level as well. The 2007 main NAEP math assessment for the eighth grade is a good example of this variation. Among students who took this exam, boys outperformed girls by two points. When broken down by race/ethnicity, however, a three-point gap favored males among white students, no significant gender gap appeared among Hispanic students, and among African American students, girls outscored boys by an average of one point. Similarly, boys outperformed girls on average on both the math and verbal portions of the SAT. Disaggregated by race/ethnicity and family income level, however, the male advantage on the verbal portion of the SAT is consistently seen only among students from low-income families and is not seen among African Americans. Gender differences cannot be fully understood without attention to race/ethnicity and family income level.

The decade following *The AAUW Report: How Schools Shortchange Girls* saw rapid gains for girls and women across many measures of educational achievement. Today, much of the popular discourse on gender and education reflects a shift in focus from girls to boys, implying that issues of equity for girls have been addressed and now it is time to focus on boys. As this report demonstrates, however, neither girls nor boys are unilaterally succeeding or failing. The true crisis is that American schoolchildren are deeply divided across race/ethnicity and family income level, and improvement has been too slow and unsteady.

This report is a call for action. It does not attempt to prescribe educational policy, nor does it provide recommendations for classroom pedagogy. A large body of research already exists on both topics, including AAUW publications listed at the back of this report and on the AAUW website. Instead, this report dispels the myth of a boys' crisis and calls for a refocused public debate on the deep divisions among schoolchildren by race/ethnicity and family income level.

Chapter 2

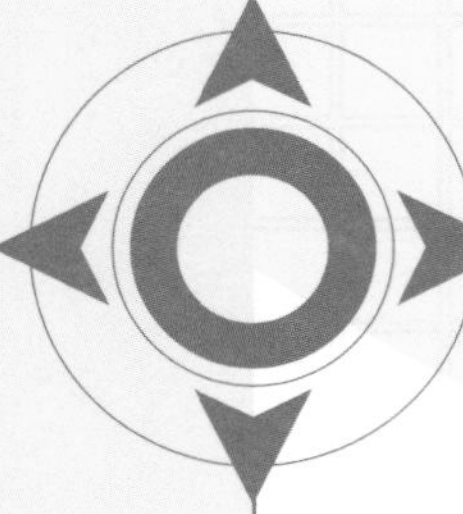

Where the Girls Are in Elementary and Secondary School

Commonly referred to as the Nation's Report Card, the National Assessment of Educational Progress (NAEP) tests U.S. students' knowledge and skills in reading, mathematics, and other subjects. This chapter uses this widely accepted barometer of student progress to consider evidence of a boys' crisis. The chapter charts trends in girls' and boys' scores on the NAEP and demonstrates that where the girls (and boys) are depends in large part on race/ethnicity and family income level.

This chapter presents data from two key NAEP assessments. The NAEP long-term trend (NAEP-LTT) assessment has been given every two to five years since the 1970s and was most recently given in 2004 to students ages 9, 13, and 17.[3] The NAEP-LTT was formulated to allow comparison of students' achievement from year to year and decade to decade and has remained essentially unchanged since its first administration (U.S. Department of Education, National Center for Education Statistics, 2007h).[4] The more recently developed main or national NAEP assessment was designed to evolve over time to reflect changes in curriculum and instruction. The main NAEP has been given every two to four years to students in grades 4, 8, and 12 in math since 1990 and reading since 1992 and was most recently given to 4th and 8th graders in 2007 and 12th graders in 2005 (ibid.).[5] The NAEP Data Explorer was used in this research to generate comparisons by gender, race/ethnicity, and family income

---

[3] Between 1971 and 2004, the sample size for the NAEP-LTT math and reading assessments for a given age ranged from 3,500 (17-year-olds taking the math test in 1996) to 26,800 (17-year-olds taking the math test in 1978). Sample sizes for a given age in a given subject were larger (between 12,000 and 27,000) before 1986. Since 1986, sample sizes have ranged from 3,700 to 7,600 (U.S. Department of Education, National Center for Education Statistics, 2005a).

[4] The next NAEP-LTT assessments will be given in 2008.

[5] In 2007, 197,700 4th graders and 153,000 8th graders took the main NAEP math assessment (U.S. Department of Education, National Center for Education Statistics, 2007g) while 191,000 4th graders and 160,700 8th graders took the main NAEP reading assessment (U.S. Department of Education, National Center for Education Statistics, 2007i). In 2005, approximately 9,000 12th graders took the main NAEP math assessment while 12,000 12th graders took the main NAEP reading assessment (U.S. Department of Education, National Center for Education Statistics, 2007j).

level; where relevant, tests of significance were performed with the NAEP Data Explorer.[6]

Overall, average scores on the NAEP tests have risen during the past few decades, especially in math.[7] Gender differences persist, however, with boys generally outscoring girls on math tests by a small margin and girls consistently outscoring boys on reading tests by a larger, but still relatively small, margin.[8]

The Gender Gap Favoring Girls in Reading Is Neither Sudden nor Increasing

Girls have consistently outperformed boys on the NAEP-LTT reading assessment since the test was first administered in 1971 (see Figure 1). Overall, the gender gap favoring girls on the reading assessment has narrowed or remained the same during the past three decades.[9] Nine-year-old boys scored higher on the reading assessment in 2004 than in any previous year, and 13- and 17-year-old boys' scores were either higher than or not significantly different from scores in the 1970s.

A Slight Gender Gap Favors Boys in Math

A gender gap favoring boys in math is small and inconsistent among younger students but more evident among older students (see Figure 2). In the nine NAEP-LTT math assessments, 9-year-old girls outscored boys in 1978 and 1982, and boys scored higher than girls

---

[6] The NAEP Data Explorer can be found on the website of the U.S. Department of Education National Center for Education Statistics at http://nces.ed.gov/nationsreportcard/naepdata. This analysis was conducted in August and September 2007.

[7] The one exception is reading scores among 17-year-olds, which declined for most groups in 2004 compared to earlier years.

[8] In a separate analysis using "Cohen's d," a widely accepted measure of effect size, Klecker (2006) shows that the gender differences in reading scores on the main NAEP exam from 1992 to 2003 fall within the "small" range for all three grades in each year.

[9] For students age 9, the gender gap on the NAEP-LTT reading assessment decreased from 13 points in 1971 to 5 points in 2004. Students ages 13 and 17 showed no difference. While scores have declined for both girls and boys on the reading assessment at age 17 from a peak in the late 1980s and early 1990s and the gender gap narrowed during the 1980s and has since widened, the gender gap in reading at age 17 was not significantly different in 2004 from what it was in 1971.

Figure 1. NAEP-LTT Reading Assessment Average Scores, by Gender, 1971–2004

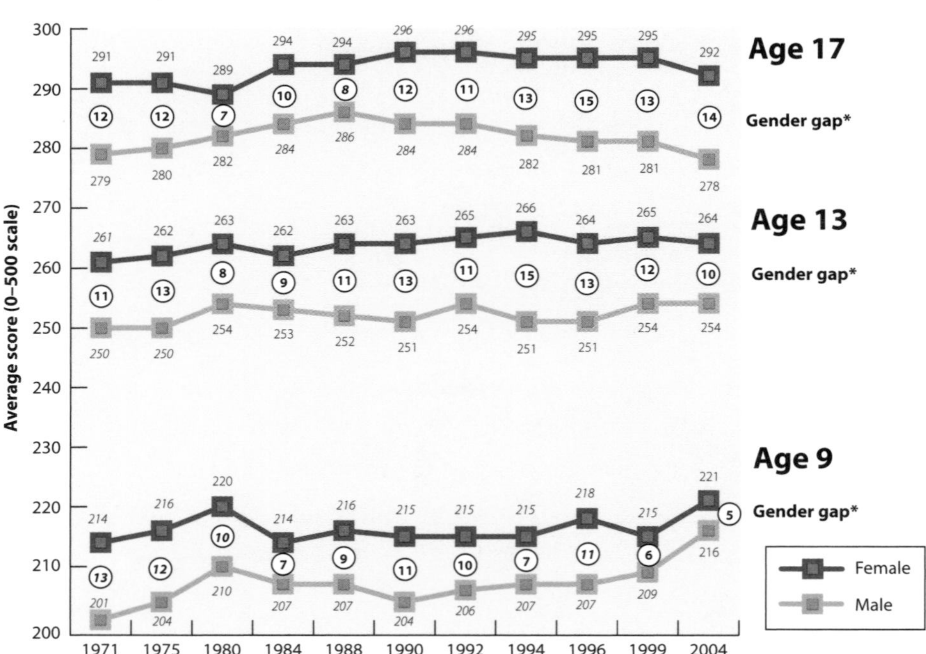

Note: **Bold** indicates significant difference between boys and girls. *Italic* indicates significant difference from 2004.

*Female average score minus male average score. Score gaps are calculated based on differences between unrounded average scores.

Source: U.S. Department of Education, National Center for Education Statistics, *The Nation's Report Card Long-term Trend: Trends in Average Reading Scale Scores by Gender*. Washington, DC: Author, 2005.

in 1996. In all other years, no difference appeared between 9-year-old girls' and boys' average scores. Among 13-year-olds, no differences appeared in six of the nine years, and boys outscored girls in 1994, 1996, and 2004. Among 17-year-olds, boys outscored girls in eight of the nine tests.

Increasing Percentages of Girls and Boys Are Scoring at Higher Levels of Proficiency

NAEP scores are reported by three levels of proficiency: basic, proficient, and advanced. **Basic** denotes partial mastery of the knowledge and skills that are fundamental for proficient work at each grade level. **Proficient** represents solid academic performance for each grade

Figure 2. NAEP-LTT Mathematics Assessment Average Scores, by Gender, 1978–2004

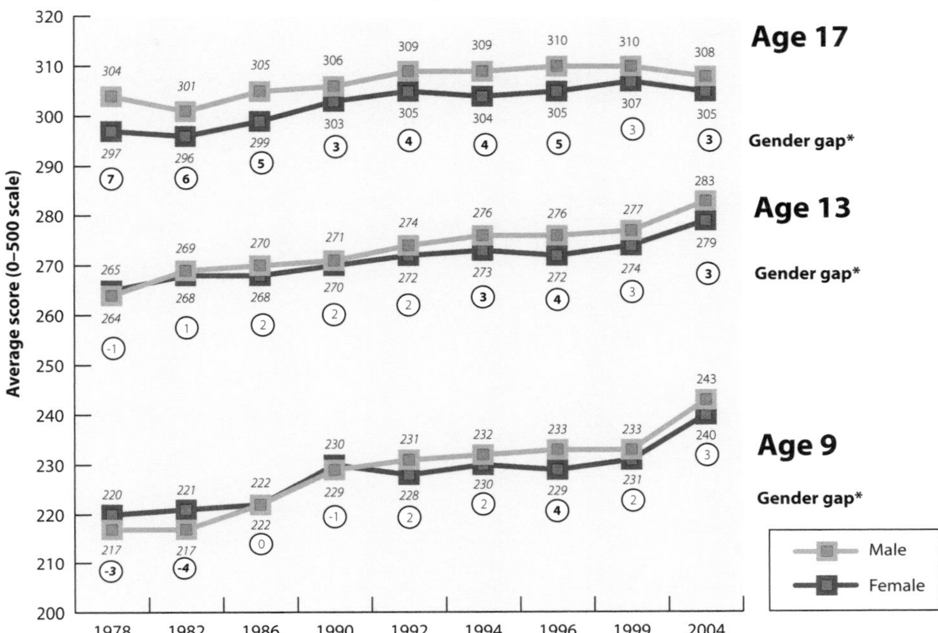

Note: **Bold** indicates significant difference between boys and girls. *Italic* indicates significant difference from 2004.

* Male average score minus female average score. Score gaps are calculated based on differences between unrounded average scores.

Source: U.S. Department of Education, National Center for Education Statistics, *The Nation's Report Card Long-term Trend: Trends in Average Mathematics Scale Scores by Gender*. Washington, DC: Author, 2005.

assessed. Students reaching this level have demonstrated competency over challenging subject matter, including subject-matter knowledge, application of such knowledge to real-world situations, and analytical skills appropriate to the subject matter. **Advanced** signifies superior performance (McGraw, Lubienski, & Strutchens, 2006; U.S. Department of Education, National Center for Education Statistics, 2007g).

Generally, more boys perform at the proficient or advanced level in math, while more girls perform at the proficient or advanced level in reading. For example, 41 percent of fourth-grade boys and 37 percent of fourth-grade girls scored at or above a proficient level on the main NAEP math exam in 2007, while 30 percent of fourth-grade boys and 36 percent of fourth-grade girls scored at or above a proficient level on the main NAEP reading exam. During the past 15 years, increasing percentages of girls and boys have scored at higher levels of proficiency in math. In reading, trends are less consistent, but where changes have occurred, they have been positive for both girls and boys. Gender gaps are often more pronounced among higher-scoring students (see Appendix A, Figures A1 through A4).

Large Gaps in Test Scores Exist by Race/Ethnicity

Consistently large gaps in NAEP test scores exist by race/ethnicity.[10] In most cases, however, these gaps have narrowed since the 1970s (see Appendix A, Figures A5 and A6). Moreover, higher percentages of all students are reaching proficiency today than in the past, including students from disadvantaged groups. In 2007, a larger proportion of fourth and eighth graders in all racial/ethnic groups scored at or above a basic level of proficiency in both math and reading than did students in the same grades in 1992 (U.S. Department of Education, National Center for Education Statistics, 2007d). Still, large disparities remain, with a majority of African American (70 percent) and Hispanic (60 percent) 12th graders scoring *below* a basic level of proficiency in math, and a majority of white (70 percent) and Asian American (73 percent) 12th graders scoring *at or above* a basic level of proficiency in 2005 (see Appendix A, Figure A7). While gaps by race/ethnicity are narrowing, progress is slow, and troubling gaps among students by race/ethnicity persist (see Appendix A, Figures A7, A8).

[10] When looking at NAEP-LTT trends, data for only African American, Hispanic, and white groups are presented because they are the only groups with sufficient sample size to lend themselves to statistically reliable comparisons (U.S. Department of Education, National Center for Education Statistics, 2005a).

Test Scores Are Closely Connected to Family Income Level

Eligibility for free or reduced-price school lunch is a commonly used indicator of family income level.[11] The proportion of eligible students is large and has been growing steadily during the past 10 years (U.S. Department of Education, National Center for Education Statistics, 2005d). In 2007, 42 percent of fourth graders taking the main NAEP math assessment and 41 percent of fourth graders taking the main NAEP reading assessment were eligible (U.S. Department of Education, National Center for Education Statistics, 2007g, 2007i).[12] When using this measure, gaps between students from higher-income and lower-income families on the most recent NAEP exam averaged 23 points in reading and 24 points in math for grades 4, 8, and 12 (authors' analysis of U.S. Department of Education, National Center for Education Statistics, 2007d) (see Figure 3).

Figure 3. Main NAEP Mathematics and Reading Assessments Average Scores, by Family Income Level, 2007*

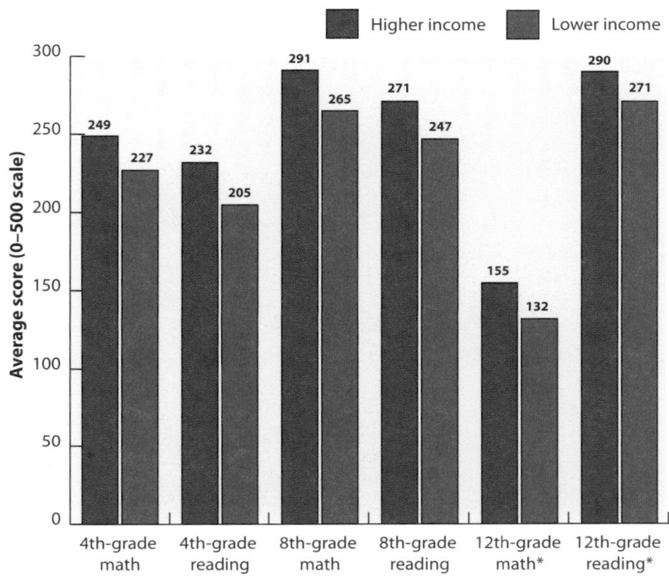

Note: Lower-income students are defined as those eligible for subsidized school lunch; higher-income students are defined as those not eligible. **Bold** indicates statistically significant difference between lower-income and higher-income groups.

*Twelfth-grade values are from 2005, the most recent year assessed. Twelfth-grade math score scale ranges from 0 to 300.

Source: U.S. Department of Education, National Center for Education Statistics, *NAEP Data Explorer*. Washington, DC: Author.

---

[11] Students from families with incomes at or below 130 percent of the poverty level are eligible for free lunch. Families with incomes between 131 percent and 185 percent of the poverty level are eligible for reduced-price school lunch, for which students can be charged no more than 40 cents (U.S. Department of Education, National Center for Education Statistics, 2007m). For the period July 1, 2006, through June 30, 2007, for a family of four, 130 percent of the poverty level was $26,000, and 185 percent was $37,000 (U.S. Department of Education, National Center for Education Statistics, 2007g).

[12] In 2005, 70 percent of African American, 33 percent of Asian American/Pacific Islander, 73 percent of Hispanic, and 24 percent of white fourth graders were eligible for free or reduced-price school lunch (U.S. Department of Education, National Center for Education Statistics, 2007m).

Students from lower-income families are less likely to score at the proficient level in math and reading (see Appendix A, Figures A9, A10). A majority of 12th graders from lower-income families (61 percent) performed *below* a basic level of proficiency on the NAEP math assessment in 2005, while a majority of students from higher-income families (66 percent) performed *at or above* a basic level of proficiency. Still, trends are positive: Higher percentages of fourth and eighth graders from lower-income families scored at or above basic, at or above proficient, and at advanced levels in math in 2007 compared to 1996 (U.S. Department of Education, National Center for Education Statistics, 2007d).

Gender Differences Vary by Race/Ethnicity

On the NAEP-LTT math assessment, an advantage for boys is found most consistently between white girls and boys, much less often between Hispanic girls and boys, and not at all between African American girls and boys. Among 13- and 17-year-olds, white boys scored higher on average than white girls on 10 of the 18 tests. On average, 13- and 17-year-old Hispanic boys outscored Hispanic girls on three of the 18 tests, and no difference existed between African American girls and boys at any age from 1978 to 2004. For 9-year-olds, no gender differences existed within any racial/ethnic group during this period (ibid.) (see Figure 4).

On the NAEP-LTT reading assessment, girls tend to outperform boys in every racial/ethnic group; however, gender differences have been most consistent among white students, less consistent among African American students, and least consistent among Hispanic students. From 1975 to 2004, white girls outperformed white boys on 29 of the 30 tests for the three age groups, African American girls outperformed their male peers on 24 of the 30 tests, and Hispanic girls outperformed Hispanic boys less than half the time—on 14 of the 30 tests (ibid.) (see Figure 5).

The 2007 main NAEP eighth-grade math assessment provides an example of how gender differences in average test scores vary across racial/ethnic groups. Among students who took this exam, a small

FIGURE 4. NAEP-LTT MATHEMATICS ASSESSMENT AVERAGE SCORES, BY GENDER AND RACE/ETHNICITY, 1978–2004

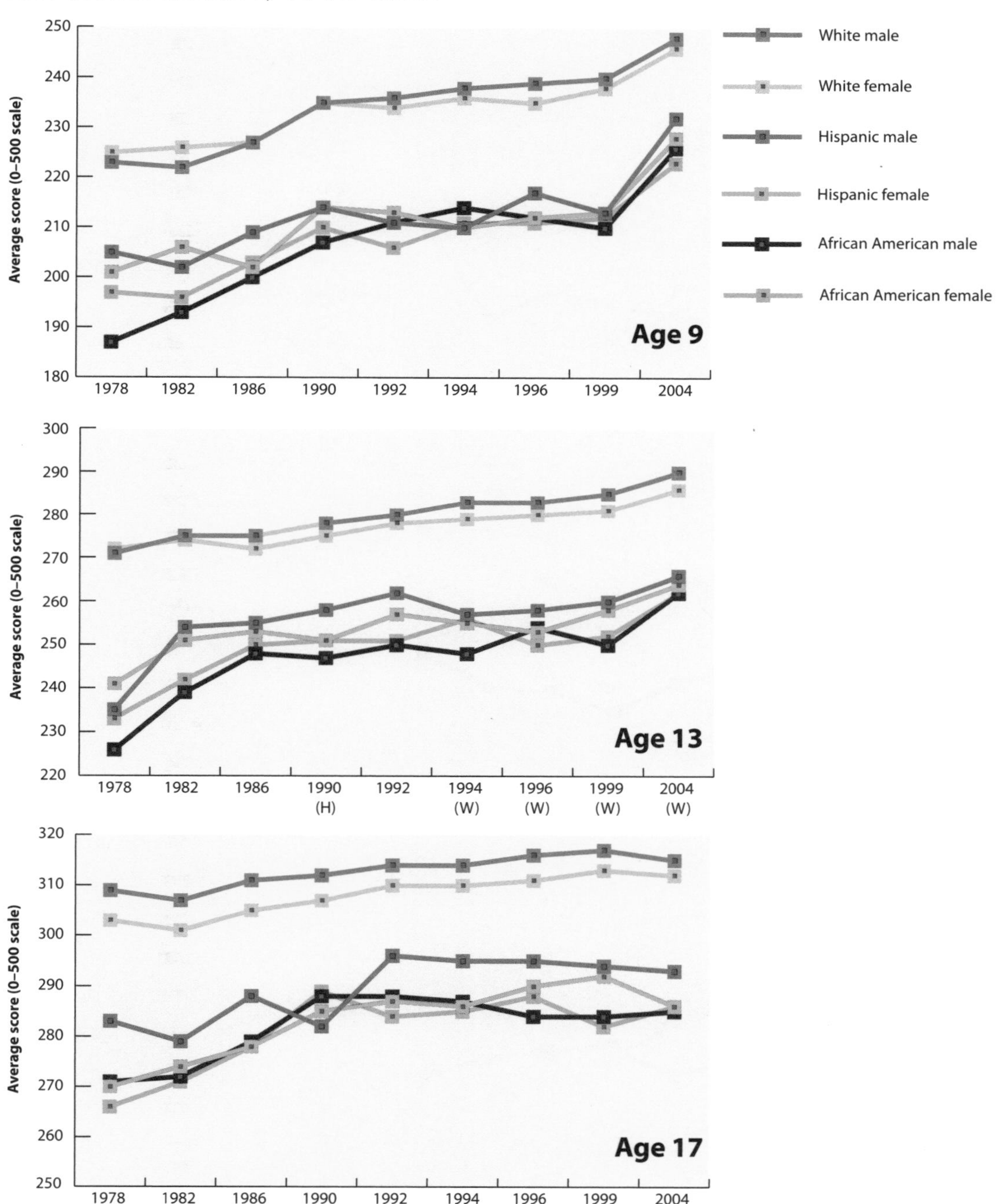

Note: A, H, and W indicate years in which there was a significant gender difference in scores among African American (A), Hispanic (H), or white (W) students.

Source: U.S. Department of Education, National Center for Education Statistics, *NAEP Data Explorer*. Washington, DC: Author.

Figure 5. NAEP-LTT Reading Assessment Average Scores, by Gender and Race/Ethnicity, 1975–2004

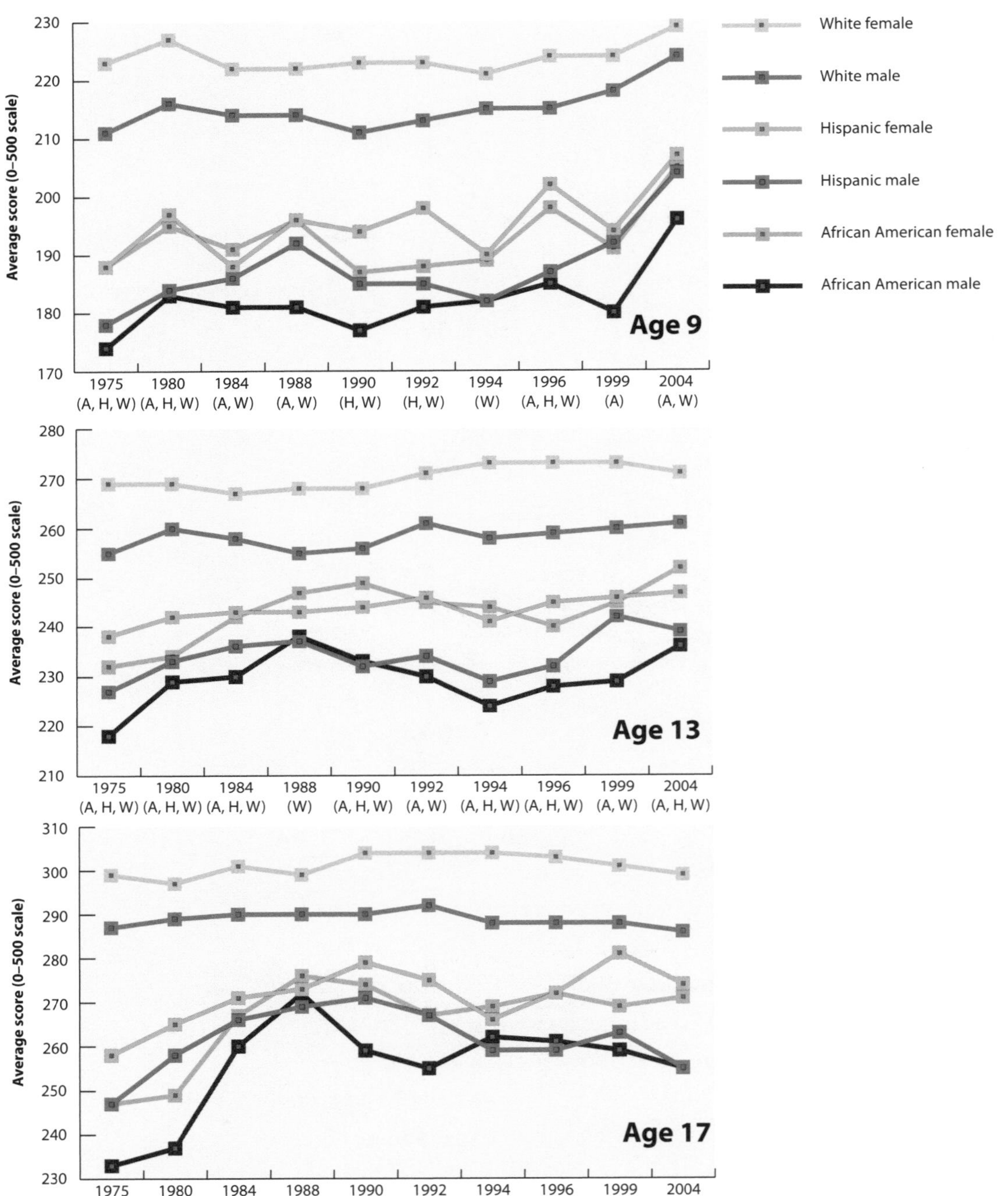

Note: A, H, and W indicate years in which there was a significant gender difference in scores among African American (A), Hispanic (H), or white (W) students.

Source: U.S. Department of Education, National Center for Education Statistics, *NAEP Data Explorer*. Washington, DC: Author.

but statistically significant gender gap of two points favored boys. When broken down by race/ethnicity, a three-point gap favored boys over girls among white students, no significant gender gap appeared among Hispanic students, and a small but significant gap favored girls among African American students (see Figure 6).

Figure 6. Main NAEP Mathematics Assessment Average Scores for 8th-Grade Students, by Gender and Race/Ethnicity, 2007

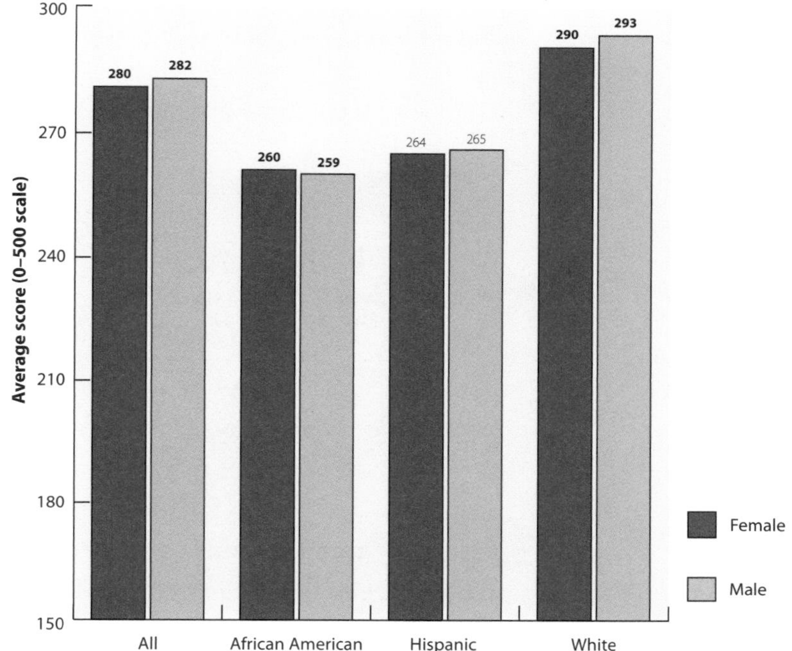

Note: **Bold** indicates significant gender gaps within racial/ethnic group.

Source: U.S. Department of Education, National Center for Education Statistics, *NAEP Data Explorer*. Washington, DC: Author.

Girls and Boys From Similar Backgrounds Have Similar Scores

Large gaps exist between white girls and boys and their African American and Hispanic peers (see Figures 4, 5, and 6). On average, African American and Hispanic girls' scores are closer to African American and Hispanic boys' scores than to white girls' scores. Similar trends appear in proficiency levels by gender within the same racial/ethnic group. Few differences are found in the percentages of girls and boys of the same race/ethnicity scoring at or above a basic level of proficiency in math on the most recent main NAEP exams in 2005 and 2007 (see Appendix A, Figure A11). On the main NAEP reading exams, however, higher percentages of girls tended to score at or above a basic level of proficiency than did boys of the same race/ethnicity for all three grades (see Appendix A, Figure A12). Still, in both math and reading, African American and Hispanic girls scored more closely to African American and Hispanic boys than to white or Asian American girls.

The story is similar for family income level. Average scores of girls and boys from lower-income families tend to be closer than do scores of girls from higher-income families and girls from lower-income families, and the same is true for boys (see Figures 7 and 8).

Math and Reading Scores Are Closely Tied to Family Income Level

In recent years, fourth- and eighth-grade boys have outscored girls within the same income group on the main NAEP math exam.[13] Average differences by gender within family income level, however, were much smaller than differences between students from different family income levels (see Figure 7).

Family income level also has a strong influence on reading scores. Scores of girls and boys from the same family income level are more similar than are scores of girls or boys from different family income levels.[14] In all main NAEP reading assessments, girls and boys from higher-income families scored higher than did girls and boys from lower-income families at all three grade levels. Within family income levels, however, girls showed a consistent advantage in reading scores, outscoring boys in grades 4 and 8 in each of the past four tests and in grade 12 in the past three tests (see Figure 8).

The effect of family income remains strong within racial/ethnic groups. For example, among white students, girls and boys from higher-income families outscored their lower-income peers in 4th and 8th grade in both math and reading and in 12th grade in math. The one exception is on the 12th-grade reading test, where no difference was found between white girls from lower-income families and white boys from higher-income families, although girls from higher-income families still outscored girls from lower-income families and boys from higher-income families still outscored boys from lower-income families (see Figure 9).

---

[13] Within family income levels, no gender difference appeared among 12th graders in the three most recent main NAEP math assessments for high school seniors.

[14] The one exception to this trend is found in the 2002 reading scores of 12th graders, where the average score of boys from higher-income families was closer to the average score of boys from lower-income families than it was to that of girls from higher-income families.

FIGURE 7. MAIN NAEP MATHEMATICS ASSESSMENT AVERAGE SCORES, BY GENDER AND FAMILY INCOME LEVEL, 2000–07*

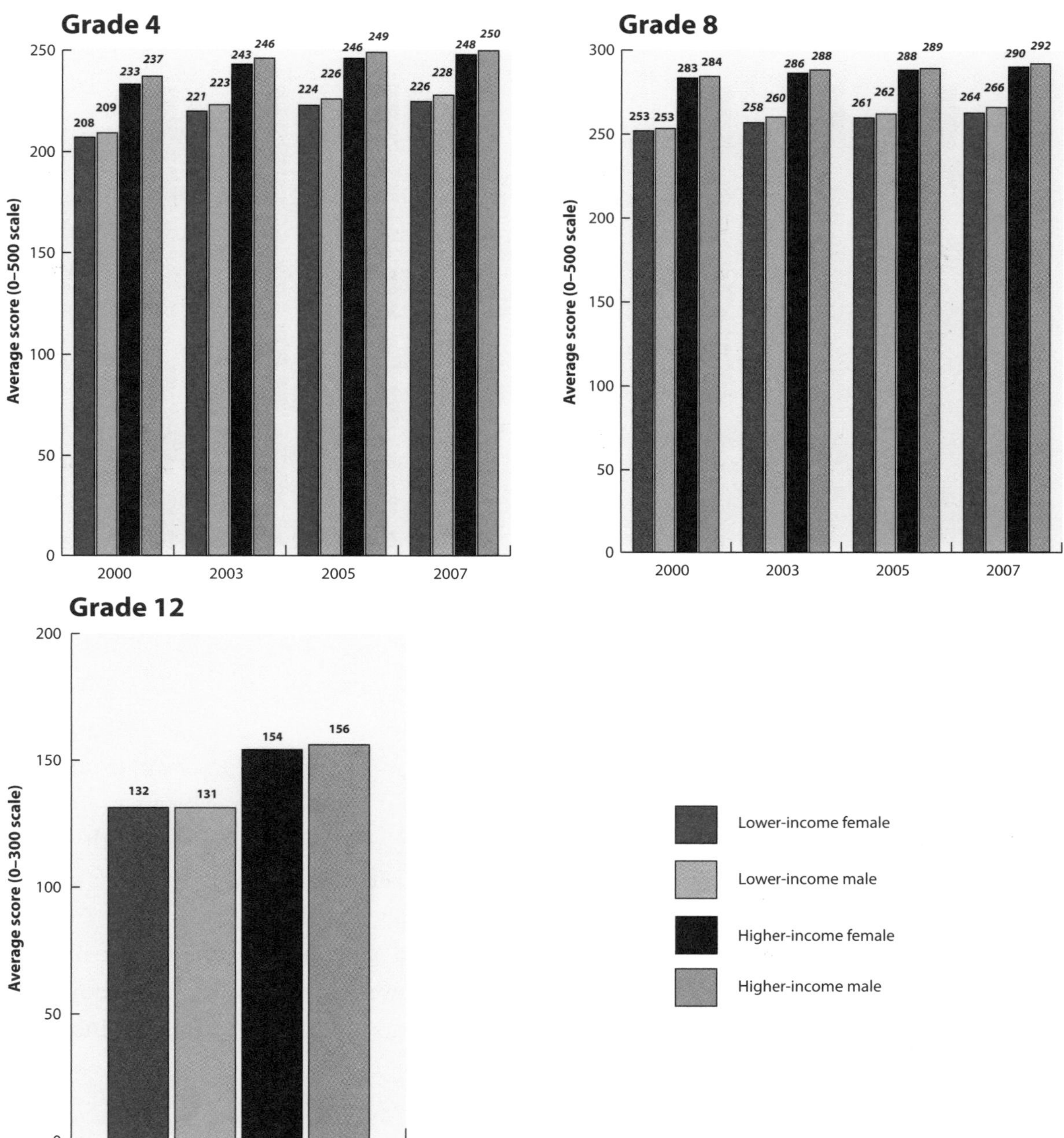

Note: Lower-income students are defined as those eligible for subsidized school lunch; higher-income students are defined as those not eligible. **Bold** indicates significant differences between higher-income girls and boys and lower-income girls and boys. *Italic* indicates significant differences between boys and girls within income level.

*The 12th-grade main NAEP was modified before the 2005 assessment; therefore, only 2005 data are shown.

Source: U.S. Department of Education, National Center for Education Statistics, *NAEP Data Explorer*. Washington, DC: Author.

Figure 8. Main NAEP Reading Assessment Average Scores, by Gender and Family Income Level, Selected Years

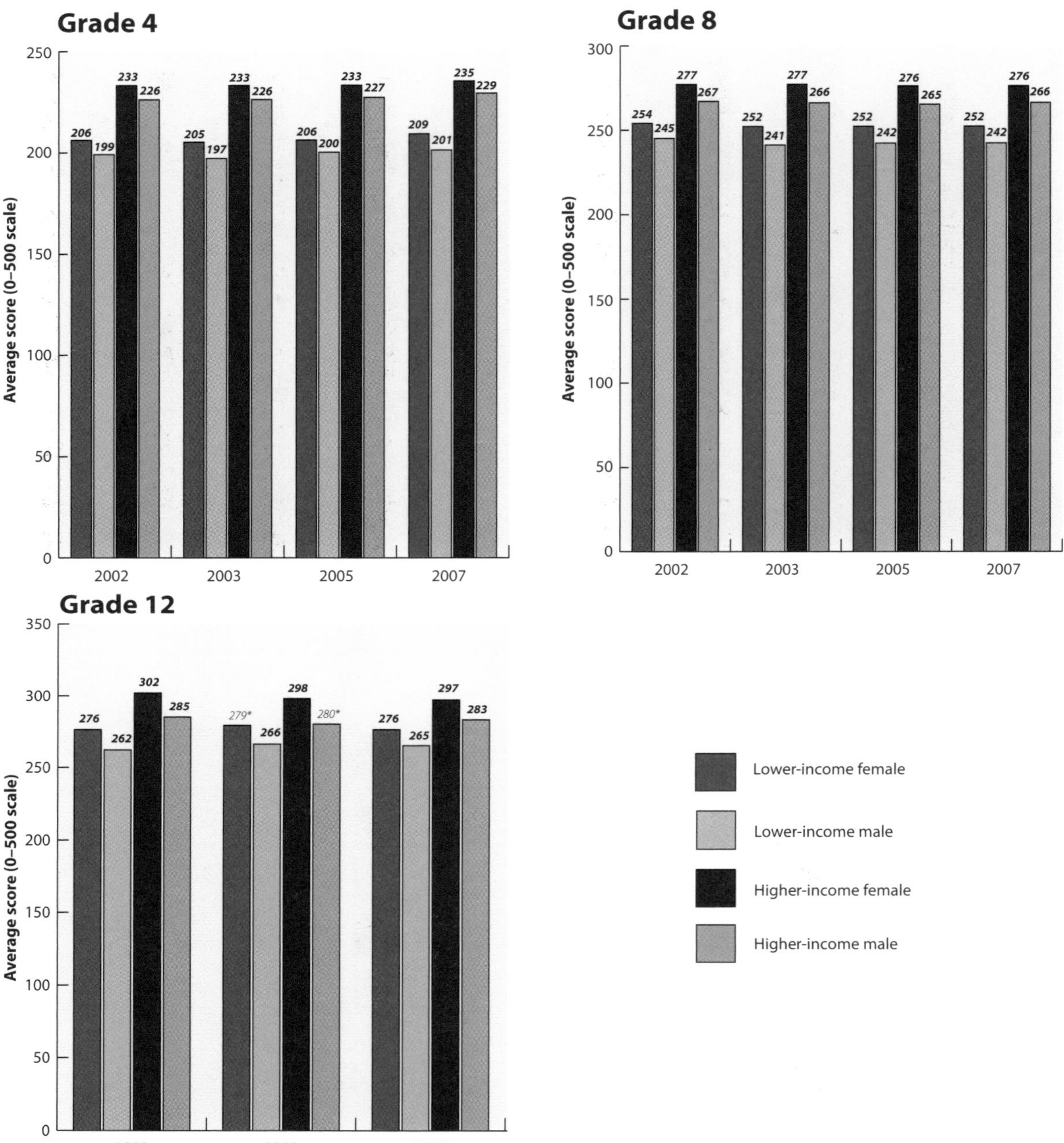

Note: Lower-income students are defined as those eligible for subsidized school lunch; higher-income students are defined as those not eligible. **Bold** indicates significant differences between higher-income girls and boys and lower-income girls and boys. *Italic* indicates significant differences between boys and girls within income level.

*In 2002 among 12th-grade test takers, higher-income boys scored significantly higher than lower-income boys but not significantly higher than lower-income girls. Lower-income girls scored significantly lower than higher-income girls but not significantly lower than higher-income boys.

Source: U.S. Department of Education, National Center for Education Statistics, *NAEP Data Explorer*. Washington, DC: Author.

FIGURE 9. MAIN NAEP MATHEMATICS AND READING ASSESSMENTS AVERAGE SCORES FOR WHITE STUDENTS, BY GENDER AND FAMILY INCOME LEVEL, MOST RECENT YEAR ASSESSED

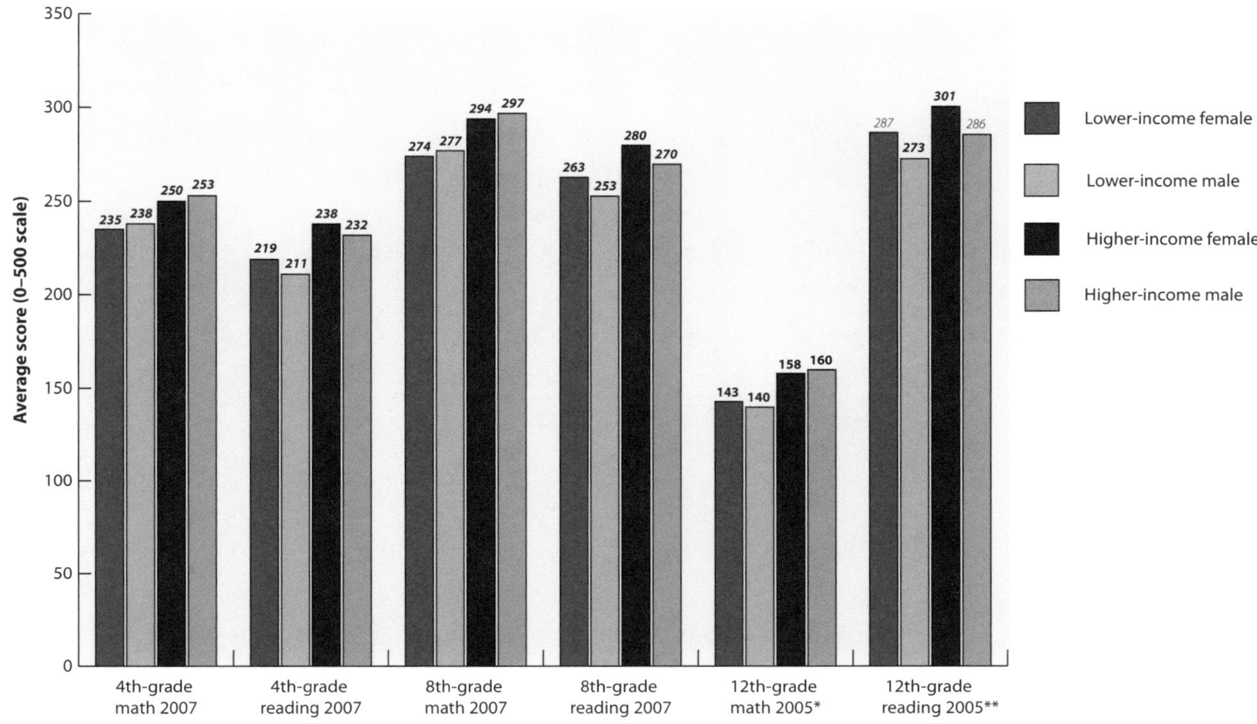

Note: Lower-income students are defined as those eligible for subsidized school lunch; higher-income students are defined as those not eligible. **Bold** indicates significant differences between higher-income girls and boys and lower-income girls and boys. Italic indicates significant differences between girls and boys within income level.

*Twelfth-grade mathematics scores are lower than those in other grades because the reporting scale was changed from 0-500 to 0-300 and the overall average mathematics score was set at 150 in 2005, the first year the new 12th-grade mathematics assessment was administered.

**Higher-income boys did not score significantly differently from lower-income girls but did significantly outscore lower-income boys. Higher-income girls outscored lower-income girls and boys in 2005 12th-grade reading.

Source: U.S. Department of Education, National Center for Education Statistics, *NAEP Data Explorer*. Washington, DC: Author.

Boys' advantage in math does not supersede the more substantial advantage of students from higher-income families over students from lower-income families. Similarly, girls' overall advantage in reading does not override the effect of family income level, although in 12th grade it comes close. The data show that boys from lower-income families perform behind the other groups in reading. Similarly, but to a lesser degree, girls from lower-income families score behind the other groups in math.

Geographic Patterns in NAEP Scores Refute a Boys' Crisis

Patterns in test scores across states provide further evidence that girls' success has not come at the expense of boys. In states where girls do well on tests, boys also do well, and states with low test scores among boys also tend to have low scores among girls. For example, test scores on the 2007 main NAEP fourth-grade math assessment by state show that the five highest-scoring states for boys—Massachusetts, New Jersey, New Hampshire, Kansas, and Minnesota—were also the highest-scoring states for girls. Similarly, three of the four states with the lowest scores for boys—Mississippi, New Mexico, and Alabama—were also three of the lowest-scoring states for girls (authors' analysis of U.S. Department of Education, National Center for Education Statistics, 2007g) (see Figures 10 and 11).

Where the Girls Are

The end of secondary school is a useful juncture to assess where the girls are. Which girls emerge from high school proficient in reading? in math? The indicators are not promising. On average, only among white girls in 2005 were at least half of 12th graders reading at or above a proficient level. In math, the numbers were less encouraging, with a clear majority of 12th-grade African American and Hispanic girls and girls from lower-income families scoring below a basic level of proficiency.

Math

A majority of 12th-grade white and Asian American/Pacific Islander girls and girls from higher-income families scored at or above the basic level of proficiency in math in 2005. A majority of African American and Hispanic girls and girls from lower-income families, however, scored below the basic level of proficiency. Only a minority of all groups of 12th-grade girls scored at or above the proficient level (see Figure 12).

Figure 10. Main NAEP Mathematics Assessment Average Scores for 4th-Grade Public School Students, by State and Gender, 2007

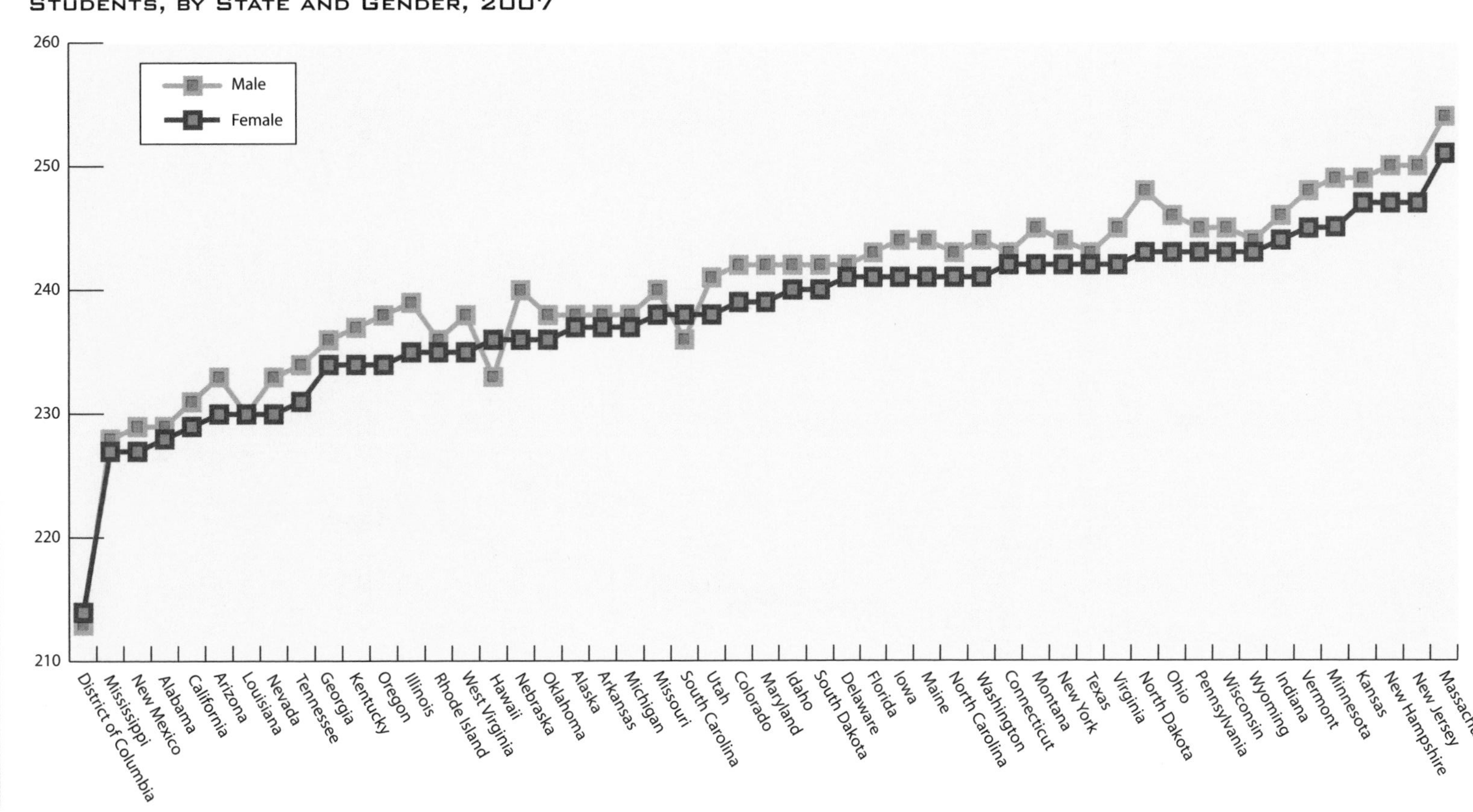

Source: U.S. Department of Education, National Center for Education Statistics, *The Nation's Report Card: Mathematics 2007*, by Jihyun Lee, Wendy S. Grigg, & Gloria S. Dion (NCES 2007–494). Washington, DC: Author, 2007.

Figure 11. Main NAEP Reading Assessment Average Scores for 4th-Grade Public School Students, by State and Gender, 2007

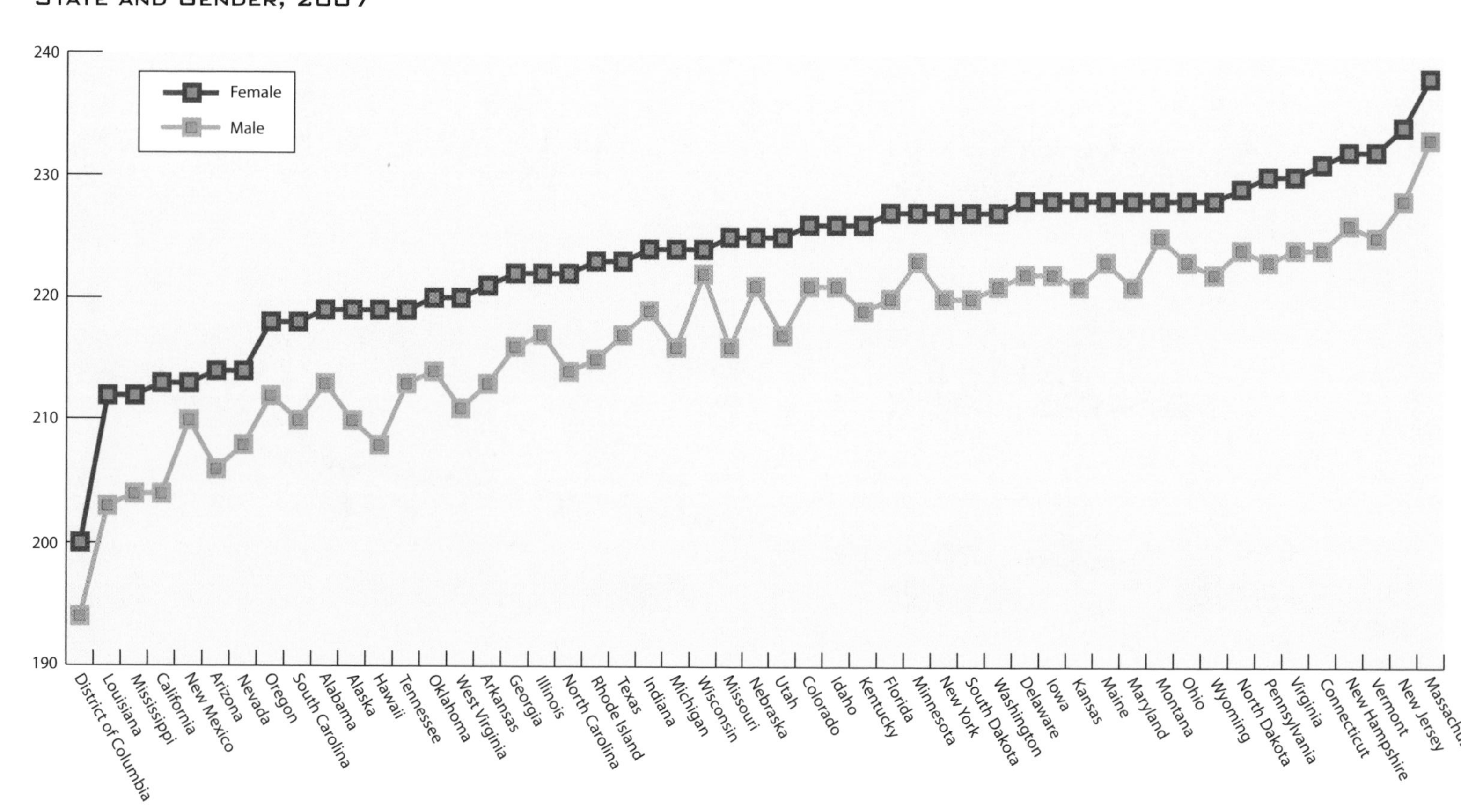

Source: U.S. Department of Education, National Center for Education Statistics, *The Nation's Report Card: Reading 2007*, by Jihyun Lee, Wendy S. Grigg, & Patricia L. Donahue (NCES 2007–496). Washington, DC: Author, 2007.

Figure 12. Main NAEP Mathematics Assessment Proficiency Levels for 12th-Grade Girls, by Race/Ethnicity and Family Income Level, 2005

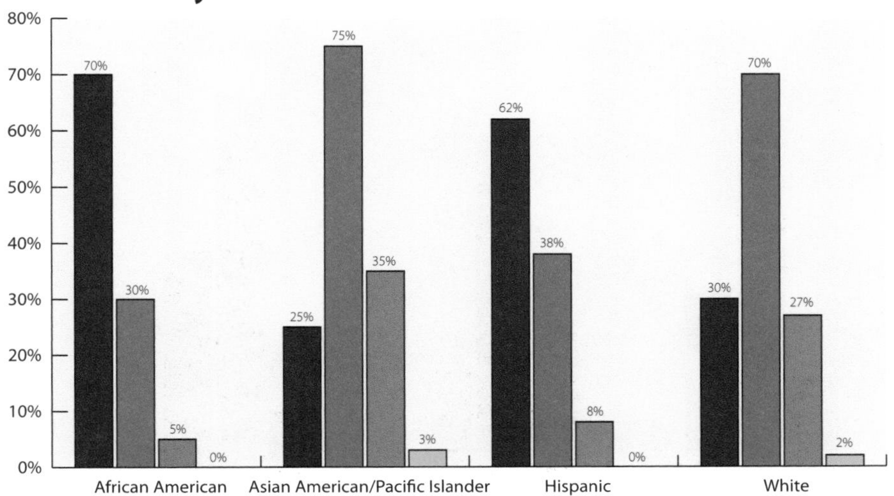

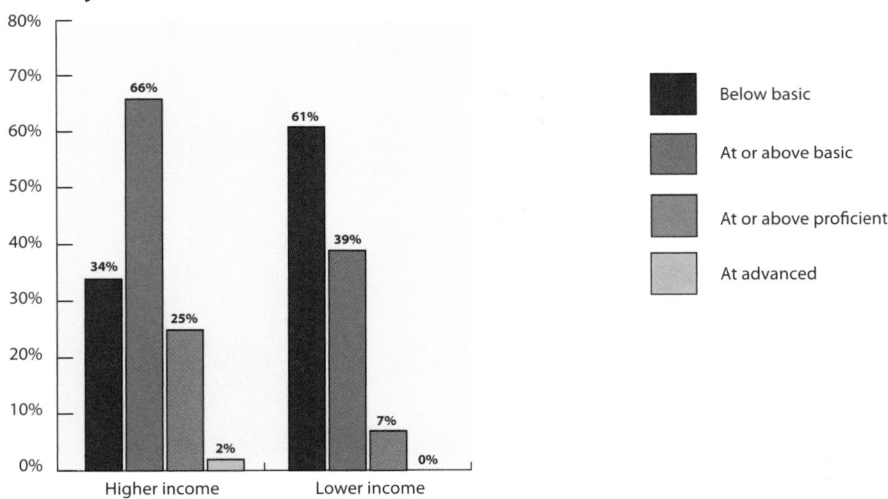

Note: Lower-income students are defined as those eligible for subsidized school lunch; higher-income students are defined as those not eligible. **Bold** indicates significant differences between higher-income girls and lower-income girls.

Source: U.S. Department of Education, National Center for Education Statistics, *NAEP Data Explorer.* Washington, DC: Author.

Figure 13. Main NAEP Reading Assessment Proficiency Levels for 12th-Grade Girls, by Race/Ethnicity and Family Income Level, 2005

Race/Ethnicity

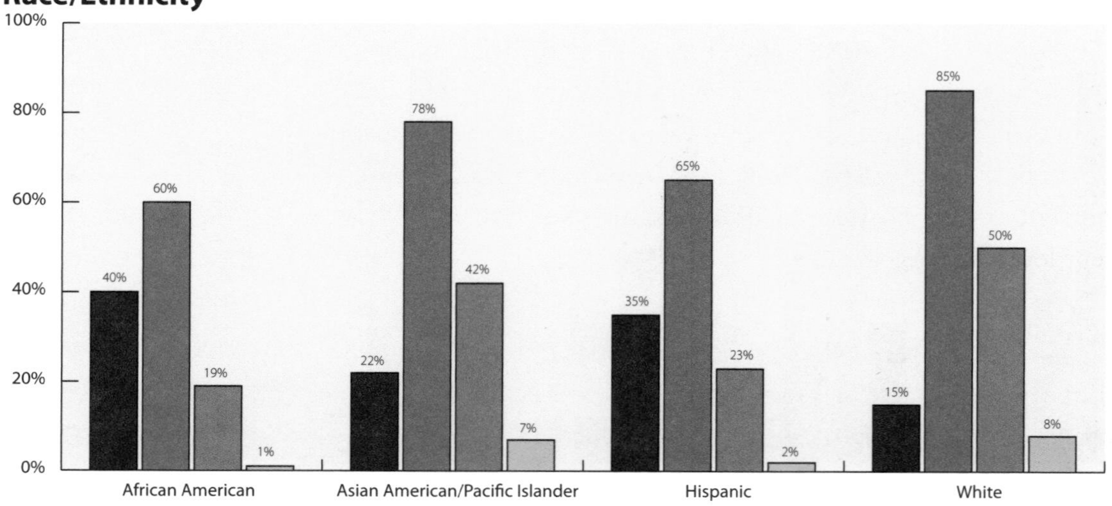

Family Income Level

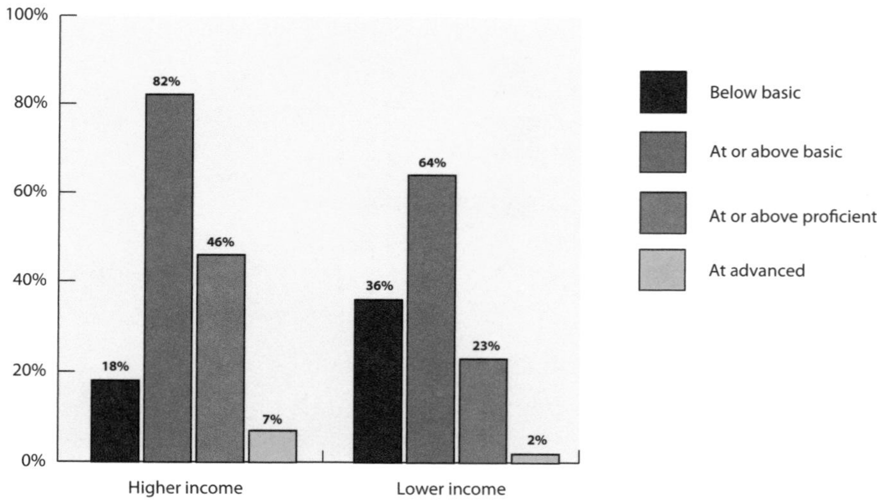

Note: Lower-income students are defined as those eligible for subsidized school lunch; higher-income students are defined as those not eligible. **Bold** indicates significant differences between higher-income girls and lower-income girls.

Source: U.S. Department of Education, National Center for Education Statistics, *NAEP Data Explorer.* Washington, DC: Author.

Reading

A majority of 12th-grade girls in all races/ethnicities and family income levels scored at or above a basic level of proficiency in reading in 2005. Half of all white girls but only 42 percent of Asian American/Pacific Islander, 23 percent of Hispanic, and 19 percent of African American girls scored at or above a proficient level. Additionally, 46 percent of girls from higher-income families compared to 23 percent of girls from lower-income families scored at or above a proficient level (see Figure 13).

Summary

Overall, both girls and boys are performing better on NAEP assessments since the 1970s, especially in math. The traditional gender differences persist, however, with boys generally outscoring girls on math tests by a small margin, and girls outscoring boys on reading tests by a larger, but still relatively small, margin. Increasing percentages of both girls and boys are performing at a proficient level in math. In reading, the percentages of girls and boys who achieve proficiency have remained about the same.

These generally positive trends, however, mask important variations by race/ethnicity and family income level. Girls from higher-income families scored higher on average than did lower-income girls in both math and reading in all three grades and all years evaluated. In addition, while disparities by race/ethnicity and family income level are not increasing, the gaps are not closing at an acceptable rate. Large differences remain among students by race/ethnicity and family income level. Gender differences occur within all groups but appear to be larger and more consistent among white students. Nevertheless, even among white students, gender differences are small relative to gaps by race/ethnicity and family income level.

Chapter 3

Where the Girls Are on the SAT and ACT

The SAT[15] and ACT are arguably the most important examinations for U.S. students. More than 80 percent of colleges and universities require either the SAT or ACT for determining admissions and financial aid awards (Sacchetti, 2006; Zwick, 2007). Among 12th graders in the 2006–07 school year, 1.5 million students, almost half of all graduating high school seniors (46 percent), took the SAT, and about 1.3 million (40 percent) took the ACT (College Board, 2007b; ACT Inc., 2007; U.S. Census Bureau, 2007).[16] Students taking the SAT and ACT are generally a self-selected group and, therefore, not representative of all of the nation's high school seniors. Nonetheless, the SAT and ACT exams play a critical role as gatekeepers to college and hence to the higher earnings associated with college and professional credentials.

This chapter examines gender differences in test scores for the SAT and ACT during a 10- to 12-year period. Because data disaggregated by gender, race/ethnicity, and family income level are not widely available for either exam, AAUW obtained data directly from ACT Inc. and the College Board (for the SAT). For 1994, 1996, 1998, 2000, 2002, and 2004, analysis was conducted on a nationally representative sample of 100,000 female and male SAT takers and significance tests were performed. For the ACT, scores were examined for the mathematics and English portions of the test from the mid-1990s through 2007. Because the data provided by ACT included all students who took the test, no significance tests were performed.

While average performance for both girls and boys has risen over time, a small but persistent gender gap favors boys on both the SAT and ACT. On the SAT, the largest gender gap occurs on the math exam (SAT-M) in favor of boys across all races/ethnicities and family income levels. Boys maintain an advantage on the SAT verbal exam (SAT-V) as well, in contrast to the NAEP exam. On the ACT, boys have slightly higher composite scores. On average, boys perform

[15] This report refers to the SAT Reasoning Test, which consists of math and verbal (critical reading) components and, since 2005, a writing section.

[16] Regional differences exist in the percentage of college-bound seniors who take the SAT or ACT or both. Students in northeastern states are more likely to take the SAT, while students in midwestern states are more likely to take the ACT (see Appendix B, Figure B1).

better on the math and science sections, and girls perform better on the English and reading sections of the ACT.

As found in the analysis of the NAEP tests in chapter 2, the gender gap for SAT and ACT students is small relative to other differences among students, and gender differences vary by race/ethnicity and family income level. Gender gaps on the SAT and ACT math exams are most pronounced among Asian American, Hispanic, and white students and are much smaller among African American students. While boys maintain an advantage on the SAT-V overall, among African American students, girls outscored boys in half of the years evaluated. When broken down by family income level, only boys from lower-income families showed a consistent advantage on the SAT-V. Girls outperformed boys within every racial/ethnic group on the ACT English exam. On average, SAT and ACT students from lower-income families tended to perform less well than did those from higher-income families, and African American and Hispanic students scored below their Asian American and white peers.

Overall, test scores on the SAT and ACT exams challenge the notion of a boys' crisis. Boys continue to hold an advantage, albeit small, on these undergraduate admissions tests. While the number of girls taking these exams has risen, so too has the number of boys.

The SAT

The SAT is intended to predict first-year college grades. Over time, the pool of SAT takers has grown and become more diverse. Just more than 1 million college-bound seniors took the SAT in 1987, with girls comprising 52 percent of test takers who indicated their gender, and almost 1.5 million students took the SAT in 2007, with girls comprising 54 percent of test takers (College Board, 2007b). During the last two decades, the number of Hispanic test takers has more than tripled, making Hispanics the largest minority group of test takers in 2007, compared to 1987, when the largest minority group was African Americans. White students made up only 55 percent of SAT takers in 2007, compared to 73 percent in 1987 (College Board, 2007b, 2007c) (see Appendix B, Figure B2).

Boys have outperformed girls on both the verbal and the math sections of the SAT during the past two decades. The gender gap on the SAT-M is larger than the gap on the SAT-V, although both gaps have narrowed slightly (College Board, 2007c) (see Appendix B, Figures B3 and B4). The recent addition of a mandatory writing section and other changes to the SAT appear to favor girls, but it is not yet clear how colleges will use the writing exam for admissions.

The gender gap in the math and verbal exams favors boys

During the decade from 1994 to 2004, boys outscored girls on the SAT-V by a margin of three to eight points. Overall average performance for both girls and boys improved during this period (see Figure 14).

FIGURE 14. SAT VERBAL/CRITICAL READING MEAN SCORE, BY GENDER, 1994–2004

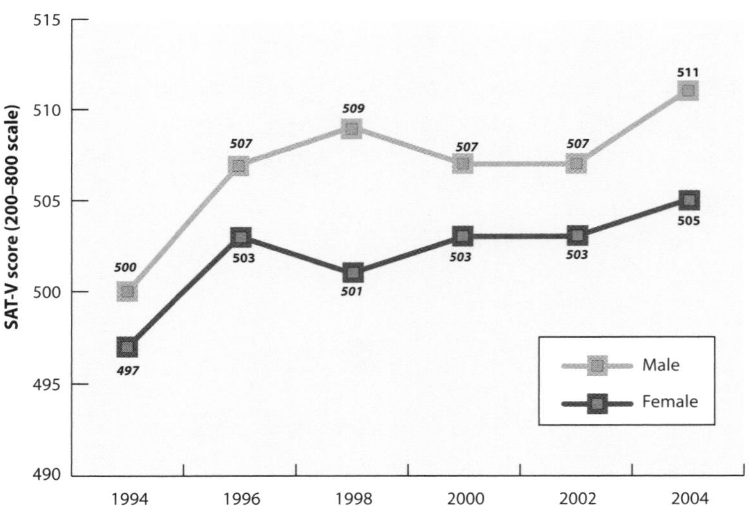

Note: **Bold** indicates significant difference between boys and girls. *Italic* indicates significant difference from 2004.

Source: AAUW Educational Foundation analysis of unpublished data provided by the College Board.

Average scores on the SAT-M improved for both girls and boys during this period. The gender gap remained fairly constant, however, with boys outscoring girls by 34 to 36 points (see Figure 15).

FIGURE 15. SAT MATHEMATICS MEAN SCORE, BY GENDER, 1994–2004

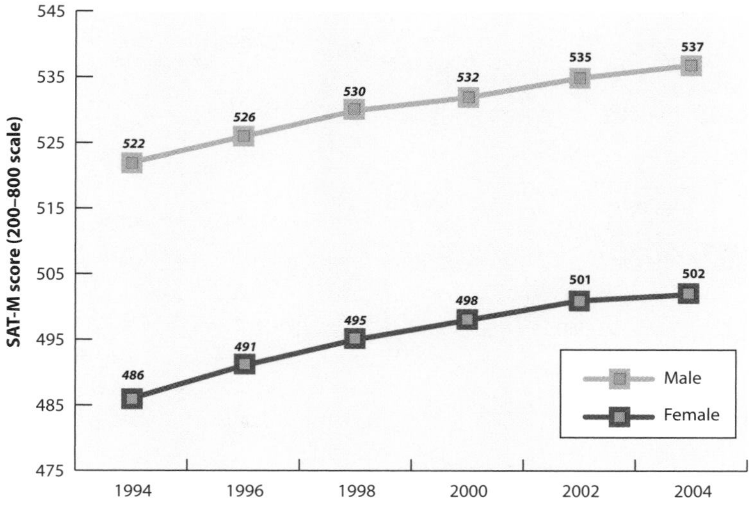

Note: **Bold** indicates significant difference between boys and girls. *Italic* indicates significant difference from 2004.

Source: AAUW Educational Foundation analysis of unpublished data provided by the College Board.

Across races/ethnicities, boys tend to outscore girls in math

In math, boys in each racial/ethnic group nearly always outscored girls in the same group, although the size of the gap varied widely. On average, the gender gap was 17 points for African Americans, about half the size of the gender gap for other races/ethnicities.[17]

From 1994 to 2004, trends varied for girls and boys of different races/ethnicities. Generally, most racial/ethnic groups performed better in 2004 than in 1994, but Asian American and white students' average scores increased more rapidly than did the scores of their Hispanic and African American peers (see Figure 16).

Gender gaps on the verbal exam vary by race/ethnicity

Trends for SAT-V scores vary more than do trends for SAT-M scores. White boys scored higher than white girls did on the SAT verbal exam in all six exam years from 1994 to 2004. A similar

[17] Among Asian American and Hispanic SAT test takers, the gender gap on the SAT-M from 1994 to 2004 averaged 36 points, while for white test takers, the gap averaged 35 points.

Figure 16. SAT Mathematics Mean Score, by Gender and Race/Ethnicity, 1994–2004

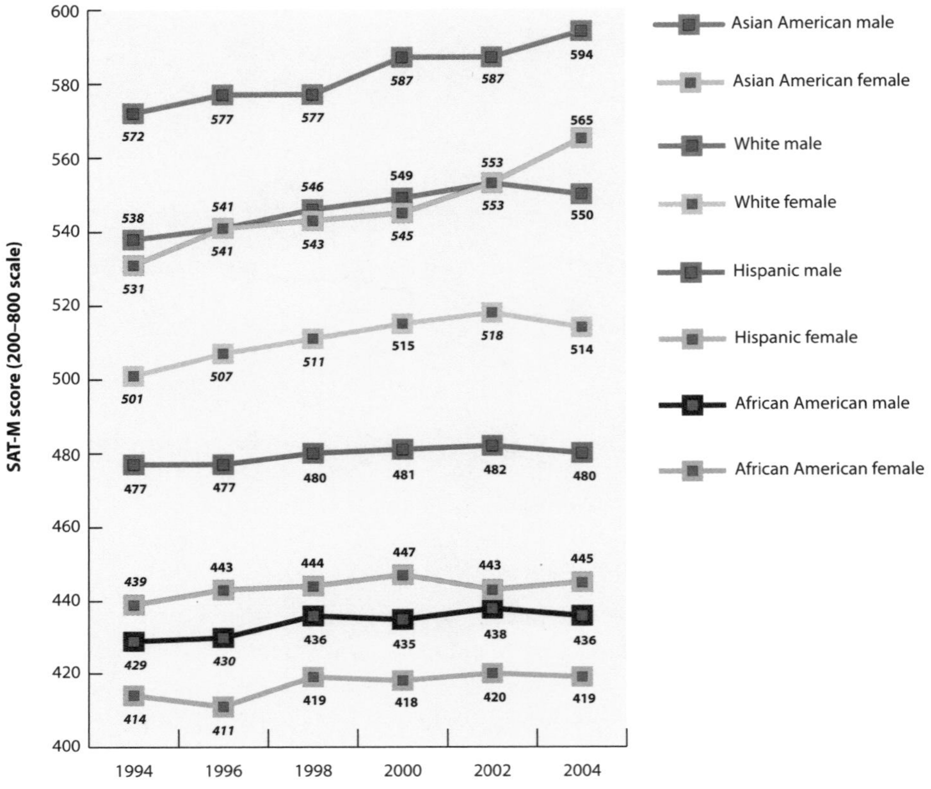

SAT-M score (200–800 scale)

	1994	1996	1998	2000	2002	2004
Asian American male	572	577	577	587	587	594
Asian American female	531	541	543	545	553	565
White male	538	541	546	549	553	550
White female	501	507	511	515	518	514
Hispanic male	477	477	480	481	482	480
Hispanic female	439	443	444	447	443	445
African American male	429	430	436	435	438	436
African American female	414	411	419	418	420	419

Note: **Bold** indicates significant difference between boys and girls within race/ethnicity. *Italic* indicates significant difference from 2004.

Source: AAUW Educational Foundation analysis of unpublished data provided by the College Board.

trend was seen among Hispanics, where boys scored higher than girls scored in every year except 2000. In contrast, Asian American girls and boys had identical average scores in 1994 and 2004, but boys had higher scores in 1998, 2000, and 2002. Among African Americans, girls performed better than boys did, with gaps in favor of girls in 1994, 1996, and 2000 and no gaps in the other years. While all groups except African American girls had higher scores in 2004 than in 1994, Asian American students' average scores increased more rapidly than did the scores of other racial/ethnic groups (see Figure 17).

Figure 17. SAT Verbal/Critical Reading Mean Score, by Gender and Race/Ethnicity, 1994–2004

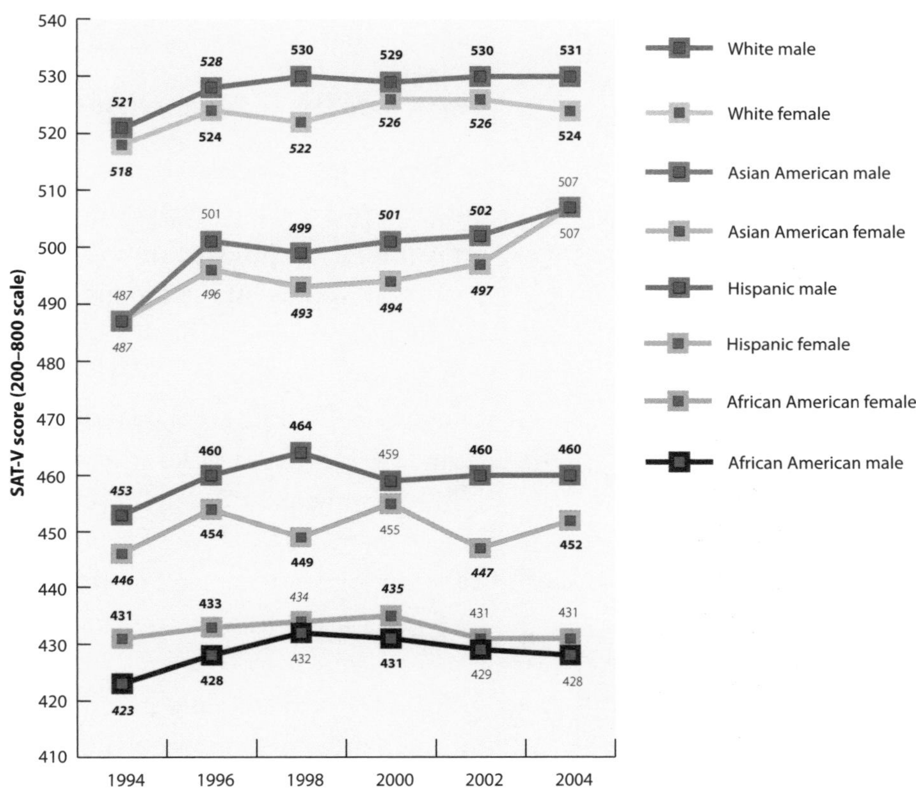

Note: **Bold** indicates significant difference between boys and girls within race/ethnicity. *Italic* indicates significant difference from 2004.

Source: AAUW Educational Foundation analysis of unpublished data provided by the College Board.

Looking at differences in SAT performance by gender and race/ethnicity highlights two important points. First, the size and the direction of the gap vary across races/ethnicities. Although Asian American, Hispanic, and white boys outperformed their female peers on the SAT-V, the reverse occurred among African Americans. On the SAT-M, boys of all racial/ethnic groups outscored girls on average, but Asian American, Hispanic, and white boys did so by a margin twice as large as that of their African American peers.

Second, on the SAT-M the improvement among white and Asian American students was two to six times as large as the improvement among African American and Hispanic students. Similarly, improvements in verbal performance were about twice as large for

Figure 18. SAT Verbal/Critical Reading Mean Score, by Gender and Family Income Level, 2004

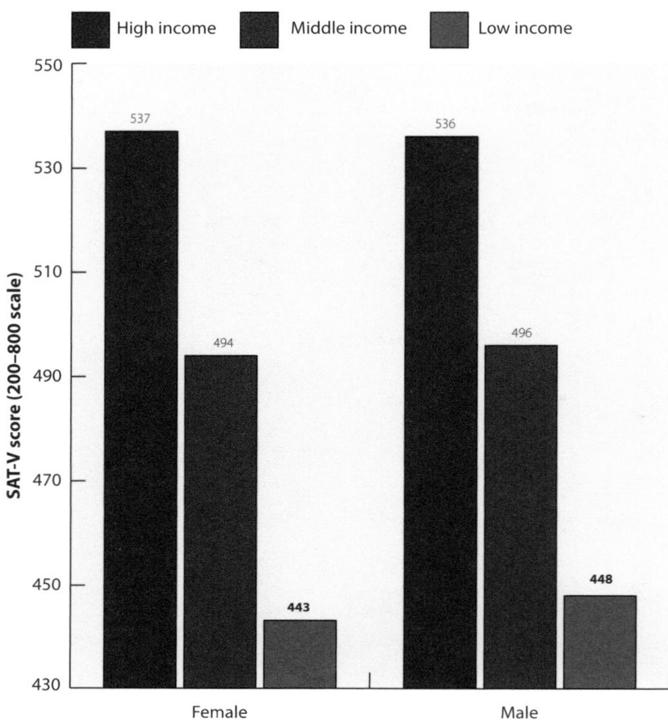

Note: Low-income students reported an annual family income of less than $30,000, middle-income students reported an annual family income of $30,000 to $70,000, and high-income students reported an annual family income of more than $70,000. **Bold** indicates significant difference between boys and girls within income level.

Source: AAUW Educational Foundation analysis of unpublished data provided by the College Board.

Asian American students as for their African American, Hispanic, and white peers.

Gender gaps vary by family income level

Gender gaps also vary among students by family income level (see Appendix B, Figures B5 and B6, for overall trends by gender and family income level). The gender gap favoring boys on the SAT-V is found in 2004 only among students from low-income families (those reporting an annual family income of less than $30,000) (see Figure 18). Among students from middle-income families (those reporting an annual family income from $30,000 to $70,000) and students from high-income families (those reporting an annual family income of more than $70,000), neither girls nor boys held a consistent advantage on the SAT-V between 1994 and 2004 (see Appendix B, Figure B5).[18]

In math, boys consistently earned higher average scores than girls earned across all family income levels in 2004, a pattern that has held true since 1994[19] (see Figure 19 and Appendix B, Figure B6).

[18] Among test takers from middle-income families, boys outperformed girls only in 1998 and 2002. Among test takers from high-income families, boys outscored girls only in 1998; in all other years, no significant gender gaps existed among students at these family income levels.

[19] Changes over time should be interpreted with caution. Because family income level categories remained the same during the 10-year period, the definition of low, middle, and high income shifts downward during that period.

SAT scores follow the same trend as NAEP scores, with students from higher-income families scoring well above students from lower-income families (see Figures 18 and 19).

FIGURE 19. SAT MATHEMATICS MEAN SCORE, BY GENDER AND FAMILY INCOME LEVEL, 2004

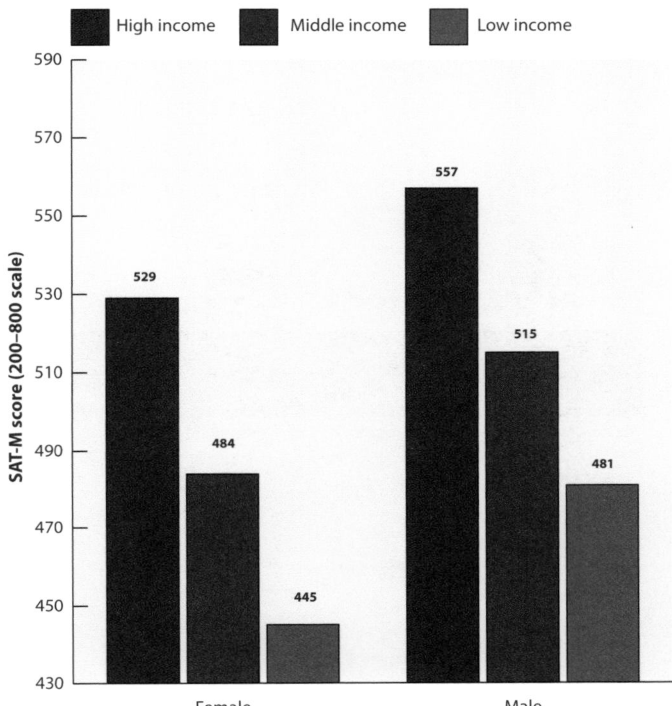

Note: Low-income students reported an annual family income of less than $30,000, middle-income students reported an annual family income of $30,000 to $70,000, and high-income students reported an annual family income of more than $70,000. **Bold** indicates significant difference between boys and girls within income level.

Source: AAUW Educational Foundation analysis of unpublished data provided by the College Board.

The ACT

Like the SAT, the ACT is meant to predict first-year college grades; however, unlike the SAT, which aims to assess general reasoning and problem-solving skills, the ACT is linked to curriculum and instructional goals. The ACT tests students in four areas—English, math, reading, and science—and it has an optional writing section. Students receive a score for each subject area and a composite score ranging from 1 to 36.

As with the SAT, the number of students taking the ACT has increased over time, and the test-taking population is becoming more diverse. Among the 1.3 million high school seniors who took the ACT in 2007, girls made up 55 percent of test takers who indicated their gender. Sixty percent of students taking the ACT indicated that they were white, 12 percent African American, 7 percent Hispanic, 3 percent Asian American, 1 percent Native American, and 17 percent indicated "other" or did not respond. African Americans were the largest minority group taking the ACT in 2007, in contrast to the SAT, where Hispanics constituted the largest minority group (ACT Inc., 2007).

Across gender and race/ethnicity, girls tend to outscore boys in English, and boys tend to outscore girls in math

On average, girls performed better on the English and reading sections of the ACT, while boys performed better on the math and science sections (see Figure 20). Boys also consistently earned higher average ACT composite scores (see Figure 21). From 1995 to 2007, the average performance for both girls and boys overall improved on the ACT English and math exams (see Figures 22 and 23).

FIGURE 20. ACT NATIONAL AVERAGE SCORE, BY GENDER, 2007

Test Takers			Scores					
Gender	Number	Percent	English	Math	Reading	Science	Composite
Female	674,636	52%	21.0	20.4	21.6	20.5	21.0
Male	544,522	42%	20.2	21.6	21.2	21.4	21.2
Gender not noted	81,441	6%	21.7	21.9	22.4	21.7	22.1

Note: Score scale is 1 to 36.

Source: ACT Inc., *ACT High School Profile Report: The Graduating Class of 2007: National.* Iowa City, IA: Author, 2007.

FIGURE 21. ACT NATIONAL AVERAGE COMPOSITE SCORE, BY GENDER, 1997–2007

	1997	1998	1999	2000	2001	2002	2003	2004	2005	2006	2007
Female	20.8	20.9	20.9	20.9	20.9	20.7	20.8	20.9	20.9	21.0	21.0
Male	21.1	21.2	21.1	21.2	21.1	20.9	21.0	21.0	21.1	21.2	21.2

Note: Score scale is 1 to 36.

Source: Unpublished data provided to the AAUW Educational Foundation by the ACT Statistical Research Department.

As with the SAT verbal exam, Asian American and white students earned higher average scores than African American and Hispanic students earned on the ACT English exam. Unlike on the SAT-V, however, within different races/ethnicities, girls consistently performed better than boys did on the ACT English exam. The largest gender gap occurred among African American students, with girls scoring an average of 1.2 points higher than boys over the 12 years. The smallest gender gap existed among Hispanic students, with girls scoring an average of 0.5 points higher than boys scored (see Figure 24).

Figure 22. ACT English Mean Score, by Gender, 1995–2007

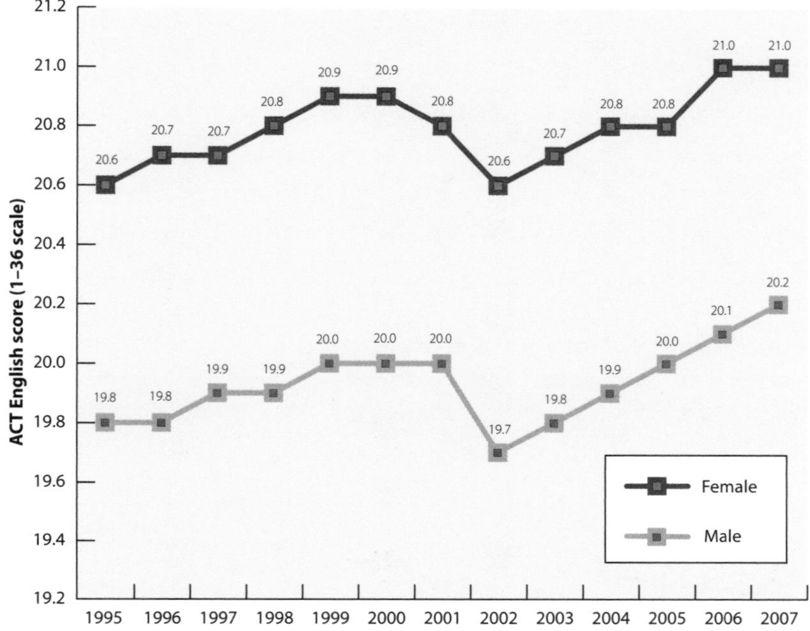

Source: Unpublished data provided to the AAUW Educational Foundation by the ACT Statistical Research Department.

Figure 23. ACT Mathematics Mean Score, by Gender, 1995–2007

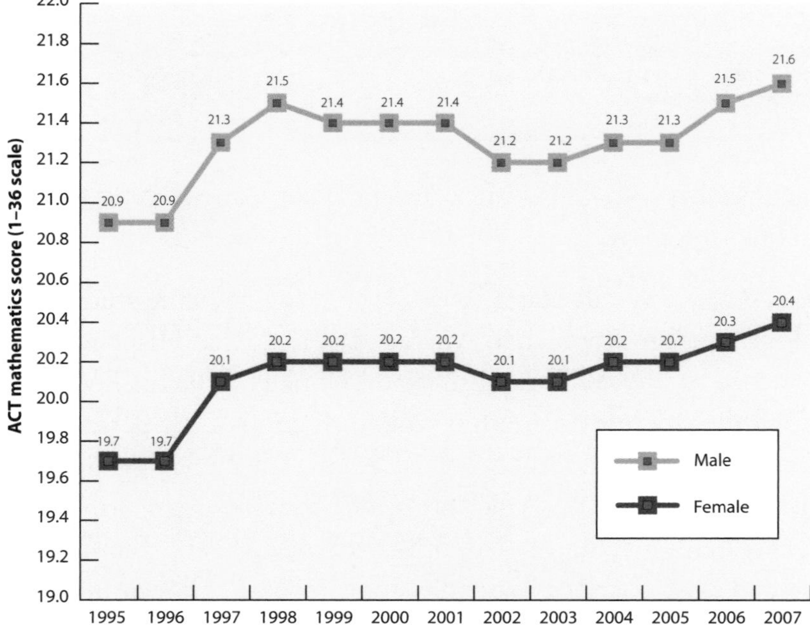

Source: Unpublished data provided to the AAUW Educational Foundation by the ACT Statistical Research Department.

Figure 24. ACT English Mean Score, by Gender and Race/Ethnicity, 1995–2007

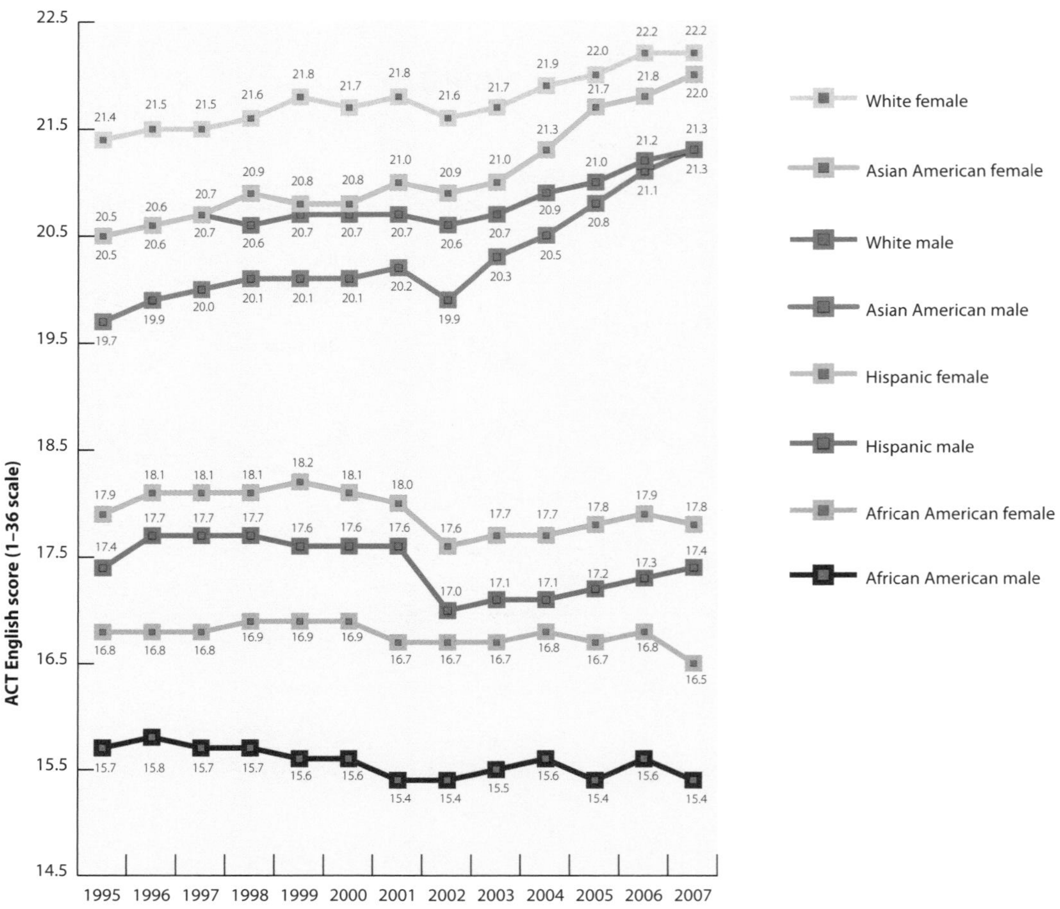

Source: Unpublished data provided to the AAUW Educational Foundation by the ACT Statistical Research Department.

Additionally, while ACT English scores for Asian American and white girls and boys improved from 1995 to 2007, scores for African American and Hispanic girls and boys either stayed the same or declined.

Asian American and white students outscored their African American and Hispanic peers on the ACT math exam over this period. Within race/ethnicity, boys consistently outperformed girls. As with the SAT-M, the gender gap was much smaller among African American students, with boys outscoring girls by only 0.2 points on average, while Asian American and white boys outscored Asian American and white girls by 1.2 points and Hispanic boys outscored Hispanic girls by 1.1 points on average (see

FIGURE 25. ACT MATHEMATICS MEAN SCORE, BY GENDER AND RACE/ETHNICITY, 1995–2007

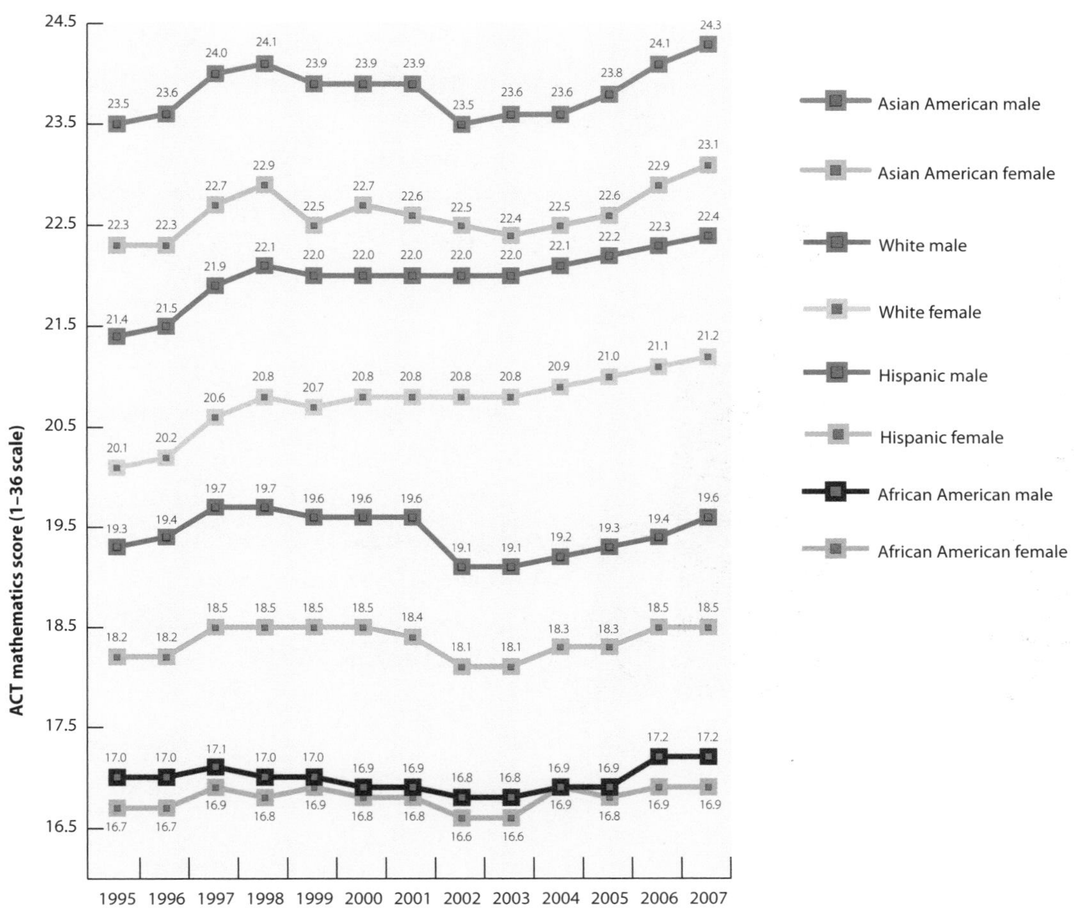

Source: Unpublished data provided to the AAUW Educational Foundation by the ACT Statistical Research Department.

Figure 25). From 1995 to 2007, average math scores for all groups rose, unlike the average scores on the ACT English exam. As with the SAT-M, however, average scores for Asian American and white students increased more rapidly than did the scores of their Hispanic and African American peers.

Scores vary by family income level

As family income increases, average scores on the ACT math and English exams rise (see Figures 26 and 27). On both exams, students from high-income families (those reporting a family income

Figure 26. ACT Mathematics Mean Score, by Gender and Family Income Level, 2007

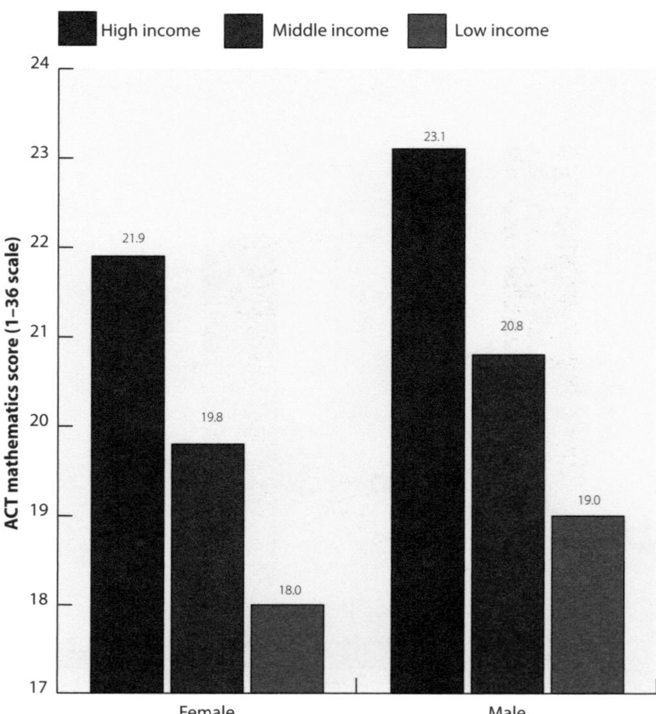

Note: Low-income students reported an annual family income of less than $30,000, middle-income students reported an annual family income of $30,000 to $60,000, and high-income students reported an annual family income of more than $60,000.

Source: Unpublished data provided to the AAUW Educational Foundation by the ACT Statistical Research Department.

of more than $60,000) consistently outperformed students from middle-income families (those reporting a family income of $30,000 to $60,000), who outperformed students from low-income families (those reporting a family income of less than $30,000) between 1997 and 2007 (see Appendix B, Figures B7 and B8). This pattern is similar to that seen in the SAT math and verbal exams (see Figures 18 and 19).

Within family income level, gender gaps on the ACT math exam were similar, with boys from each family income level outscoring girls by approximately one point on average from 1997 to 2007 (see Figure 26 and Appendix B, Figure B7).

On the ACT English exam, the gender gaps were similar within family income levels, with gaps slightly widening as income increased. Between 1997 and 2007, girls from all family income levels outscored their male peers (see Figure 27 and Appendix B, Figure B8).

Why Is There a Gender Gap?

Several explanations have been offered to make sense of the persistent gender differences in performance on standardized tests like the SAT and ACT, including test bias, biological gender differences, test anxiety, peer relationships, and differences in course taking (College Board, 2007c; Young & Fisler, 2000). Perhaps the most widely accepted explanation is that more girls than boys choose to take these college-entrance exams. The group of girls, therefore, is less "selective," and the gender gap, in part, reflects this bias (College

Board, 1988; Young & Fisler, 2000). Research on the effect of the difference in populations of girls and boys has produced mixed results (ibid.).

Recent experiences, however, support the self-selection hypothesis. Since 2002, all high school students in Illinois and Colorado have been required to take the ACT as part of statewide testing mandates. In both states, the male advantage on the composite score disappeared, and in subsequent years a small female advantage has emerged (ACT Inc., 2005b). A similar result occurred in 2007, when Maine became the first state to require all high school seniors to take the SAT (Cech, 2007). Although overall average scores for both girls and boys fell in all three subject areas compared to the 2006 scores, the gender gap on the verbal section was reversed. High school senior boys had a five-point advantage over girls on the SAT-V in 2006, but girls had a 13-point advantage in 2007. Additionally, although boys still outperformed girls on the SAT-M, the gender gap was reduced from 38 points in 2006 to 12 points in 2007. Girls also widened their advantage in the writing section, where the gap grew from 13 points in 2006 to 32 points in 2007 (Cech, 2007; College Board, 2007a). These results, though limited, support the argument that test-taking population differences can partially account for the gender gap in SAT and ACT performance.

Figure 27. ACT English Mean Score, by Gender and Family Income Level, 2007

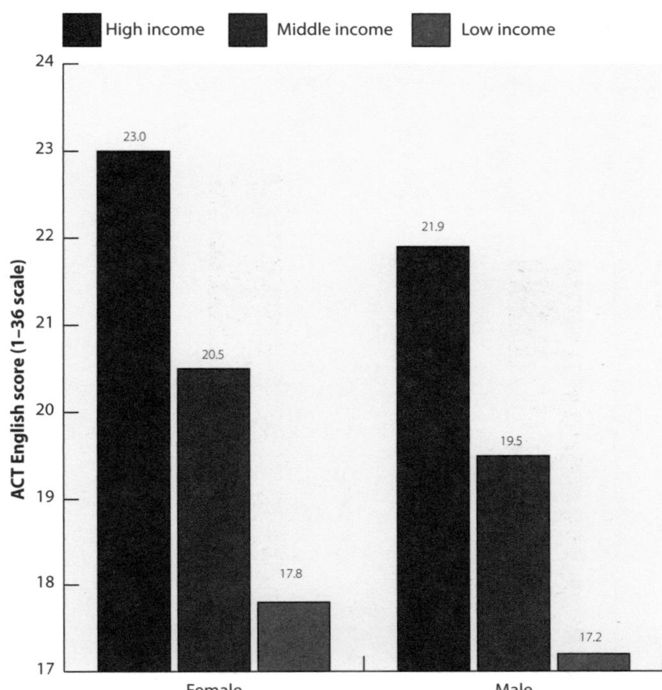

Note: Low-income students reported an annual family income of less than $30,000, middle-income students reported an annual family income of $30,000 to $60,000, and high-income students reported an annual family income of more than $60,000.

Source: Unpublished data provided to the AAUW Educational Foundation by the ACT Statistical Research Department.

Where the Girls Are

Generally, girls' average scores on the SAT and ACT have either improved or held steady in recent years. Average scores on both the SAT-M and SAT-V improved among all races/ethnicities (with the exception of African American girls, who showed no change in verbal scores). White and Asian American girls consistently outscored their Hispanic and African American peers. Asian American girls' scores on the math and verbal portions of the SAT improved especially rapidly.

On the ACT English exam, Asian American and white girls' scores increased from 1995 to 2007, while African American and Hispanic girls' scores declined slightly. Girls' scores in all racial/ethnic groups increased on the ACT math exam during this period, but Asian American and white girls' scores increased two to five times as fast as those of their African American and Hispanic peers.

As found in the analysis of the NAEP scores, student performance on the SAT and ACT exams is strongly related to family income level, with girls from higher-income families consistently outscoring girls from lower-income families. While girls are doing better overall than ever before, many Hispanic and African American girls and girls from lower-income families are not doing as well as their peers.

Analysis of trends in college entrance exams provides no evidence of a boys' crisis. Across the board, scores on both the SAT and ACT have improved or held steady from 1994 to 2004, with boys retaining a small edge in math on both exams. Girls are more likely than boys to take college entrance exams, but the growing number of girls taking these exams has not come at the expense of boys. More boys and young men are taking college entrance exams than ever before.

Chapter 4

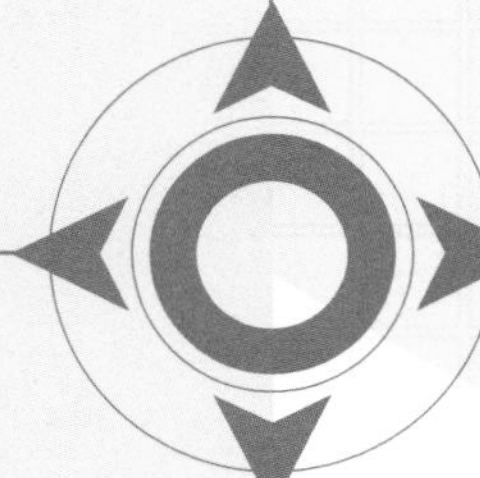

Where the Girls Are in High School and College

Girls' and women's achievements in high school and college have not come at the expense of boys or men. Boys' grades in high school have risen during the past 15 years, and more young men are graduating from high school and college than ever before. Overall, the past 15 years have been a period of increasing achievement for both young women and young men.

Race/ethnicity and family income level are important factors in high school and college achievement regardless of gender. The story is familiar: White children are more likely to graduate from high school and attend and graduate from college than are their African American and Hispanic peers. Likewise, children from lower-income families are less likely than children from higher-income families to graduate from high school. Students from lower-income families were approximately five times more likely than students from higher-income families to drop out of high school in 2003 (U.S. Department of Education, National Center for Education Statistics, 2006a). Women and men from lower-income families are also less likely to attend, much less graduate from, college (U.S. Department of Education, National Center for Education Statistics, 2006b).

FIGURE 28. HIGH SCHOOL GRADE POINT AVERAGE, BY GENDER, 1990–2005

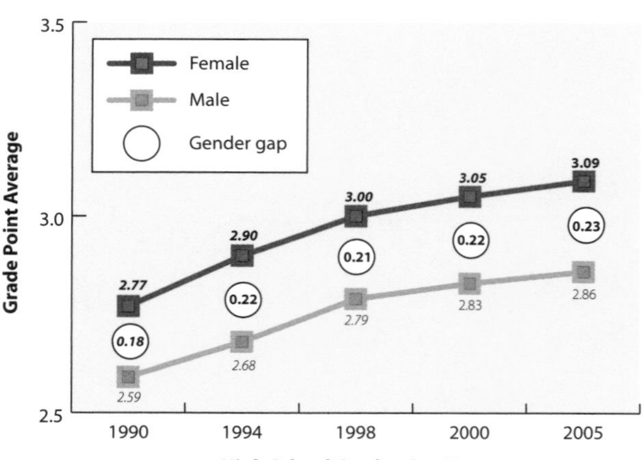

Note: **Bold** indicates significant difference from average boys' GPA. *Italic* indicates significant difference from 2005.

Source: U.S. Department of Education, National Center for Education Statistics, *The Nation's Report Card: America's High School Graduates: Results From the 2005 NAEP High School Transcript Study,* by C. Shettle, S. Roey, J. Mordica, R. Perkins, C. Nord, J. Teodorovic, J. Brown, M. Lyons, C. Averett, & D. Kastberg (NCES 2007-467). Washington, DC: U.S. Government Printing Office, 2007.

Where the Girls Are in High School

Boys and girls are both earning higher grade point averages in high school, with girls slightly outperforming boys (see Figure 28). Girls' higher GPA does not reflect enrollment in easier classes; in fact, girls earn more credits than boys earn in high school math and science and have a higher combined GPA in these courses (U.S. Department of Education, National Center for Education Statistics, 2007f).

Most young women and men graduate from high school, with a small gap favoring women. In 2006, according to the U.S. Census Bureau, 88.5 percent of women ages 25 to 29 had graduated from high school, compared to 84.4 percent of males, with a larger gender gap among Hispanics (see Figures 29 and 30). Differences exist among young women by race/ethnicity, and in this case they are substantial. Of women ages 25 to 29 in 2006, 95 percent of white women were high school graduates, but only 88 percent of African American and 67 percent of Hispanic women were high school graduates. This difference may be explained in part by immigration.

Figure 29. Percentage of 25- to 29-Year-Olds Who Completed High School, by Gender and Race/Ethnicity, 2006

	Overall	Male	Female	Gender Gap
African American	86.3%	84.2%	88.0%	**3.8**
Hispanic	63.2%	60.5%	66.6%	**6.1**
White	93.4%	92.3%	94.6%	**2.3**
Total	86.4%	84.4%	88.5%	**4.1**

Note: **Bold** indicates significant gender gap. All differences in graduation rates between racial/ethnic groups (male, female, and overall) are statistically significant.

Source: U.S. Department of Education, National Center for Education Statistics, *The Condition of Education 2007* (NCES 2007-064). Washington, DC: Author, 2007.

Research based on school administrative data shows much lower graduation rates than those reported by the Census Bureau, including Greene and Winters (2002), whose methods and results have been widely cited and are accepted by the National Governors Association. In part, these numbers are lower because the researchers did not include general equivalency diploma (GED)

Figure 30. Percentage of 25- to 29-Year-Olds Who Completed High School, by Gender and Race/Ethnicity, 1971–2006

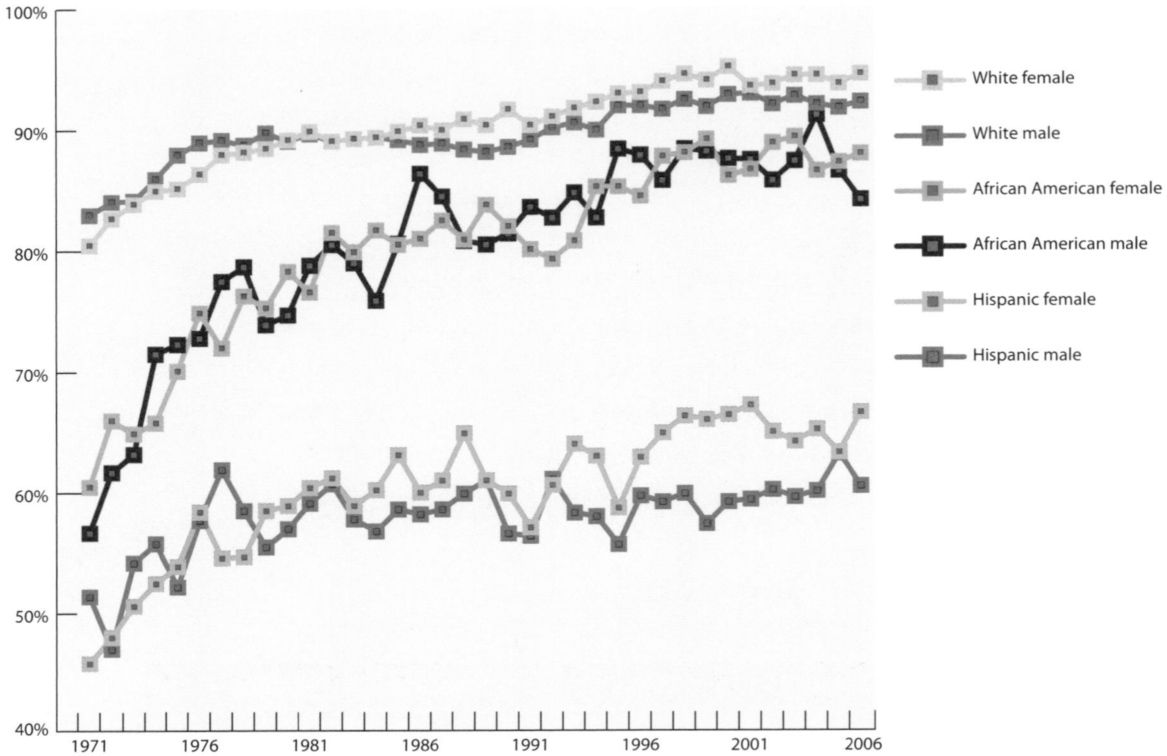

Source: U.S. Department of Education, National Center for Education Statistics, *The Condition of Education 2007* (NCES 2007-064). Washington, DC: Author, 2007.

recipients or students who take more than four years to graduate (Greene & Winters, 2005).[20, 21]

---

[20] Data on high school graduation and dropout rates vary widely by source. Federal law requires states to report on-time graduation rates to meet accountability requirements, but states use a variety of methods to calculate their rates, making comparisons difficult. Critics of the U.S. Census Bureau data on high school graduation rates (used in Figures 29 and 30) argue that the data are misleading because they are self-reported; exclude members of the military living in barracks, the incarcerated, and other institutionalized populations; and include GED recipients as well as high school graduates. Additionally, Census Bureau figures include recent immigrants who may have never attended school in the United States.

[21] The high school graduation rate gaps between whites and other races/ethnicities grow if only students who graduate in four years are counted. A larger proportion of students from races/ethnicities other than white take more than four years to graduate and earn GEDs. The National Education Longitudinal Study of 1988 estimates that among a nationally representative sample of individuals in their mid-twenties, 13.6 percent of African Americans, 9.4 percent of Hispanics, and 4.9 percent of whites held GEDs in 2000 (U.S. Department of Education, National Center for Education Statistics, 2002).

Despite a lack of consensus on actual high school graduation rates, most education researchers agree that rates have improved over time and have generally leveled off in the last decade (Greene & Winters, 2005; Mishel & Roy, 2006). Most researchers also agree that historically disadvantaged groups—African American and Hispanic students and students from lower-income families—have lower graduation rates than do white and Asian American students and students from higher-income families. Research consistently shows that across all racial/ethnic groups, a higher percentage of women than men graduate.

In summary, across all races/ethnicities a higher percentage of girls than boys graduate from high school. Yet, graduation rates for boys are generally improving, and boys as well as girls are earning higher GPAs. Clearly girls' achievements in high school have not come at the expense of boys.

Where the Girls Are in College

One of the statistics most often cited to support assertions that a boys' crisis in education exists is the increasing percentage of women earning college degrees. Women have earned more bachelor's degrees than men since 1982 (see Figure 31). Women earned 57 percent of bachelor's degrees, the majority of associate's and master's degrees, and about half of first professional and doctoral degrees (50 and 49 percent, respectively) in 2004–05 (see Figure 32). The increasing numbers of women in college have not come at the expense of men. More men are earning college degrees today in the United States than at any time in history. During the past 35 years, the college-educated population has greatly expanded: The number of bachelor's degrees awarded annually rose 82 percent, from 792,316 in 1969–70 to 1,439,264 in 2004–05 (U.S. Department of Education, National Center for Education Statistics, 2007b).

Researchers point to a number of factors to account for women's increased college participation, including changing work and family expectations of young women, demand for college graduates in the labor market, and access to birth control (Goldin, Katz, & Kuziemko, 2006). Evidence also shows that the benefits of a col-

Figure 31. Number of Bachelor's Degrees Conferred, by Gender, 1969–70 to 2004–05

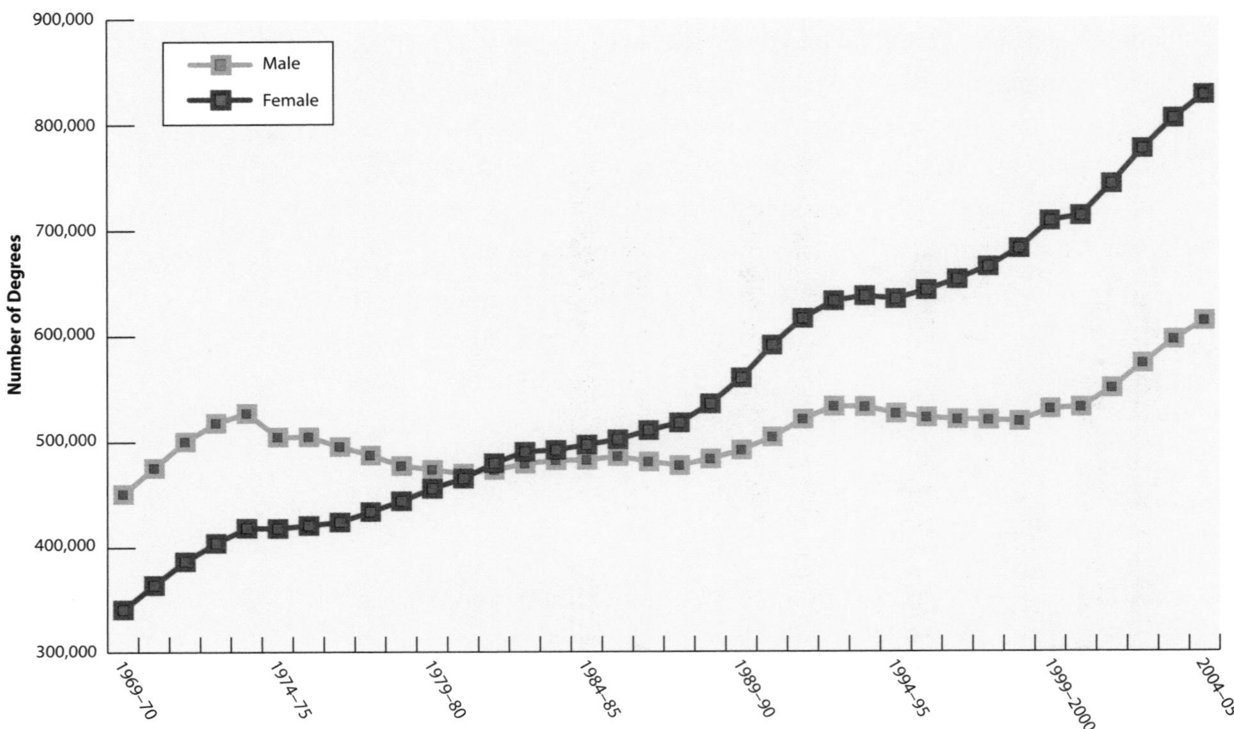

Source: U.S. Department of Education, National Center for Education Statistics, *Digest of Education Statistics 2006* by Thomas D. Snyder, Sally A. Dillow, & Charlene M. Hoffman (NCES 2007-017). Washington DC: U.S. Government Printing Office, 2007, Table 251.

lege degree in terms of increased personal earnings, improved family standard of living, and the probability of avoiding poverty are higher for women than for men (DiPrete & Buchmann, 2006).[22] A college degree provides women with a measure of insurance against poverty because college-educated women earn higher wages, have a lower rate of out-of-marriage childbearing, and have a lower risk of divorce than do women who do not earn college degrees (ibid.). Other studies have shown that education not only increases a woman's skills and productivity, as it does men's, but also appears to reduce the gap

[22] Part of the reason for this may be that a college-educated woman's probability of marrying a college-educated man is much higher than that of a woman who has not attended college. The combination of a woman's increased earnings due to her degree along with her college-educated husband's increased earnings result in a more significant return on a college education for a woman than just her earnings increase alone (DiPrete & Buchmann, 2006; Goldin, 1992).

FIGURE 32. PERCENTAGE OF DEGREES EARNED BY WOMEN, SELECTED YEARS

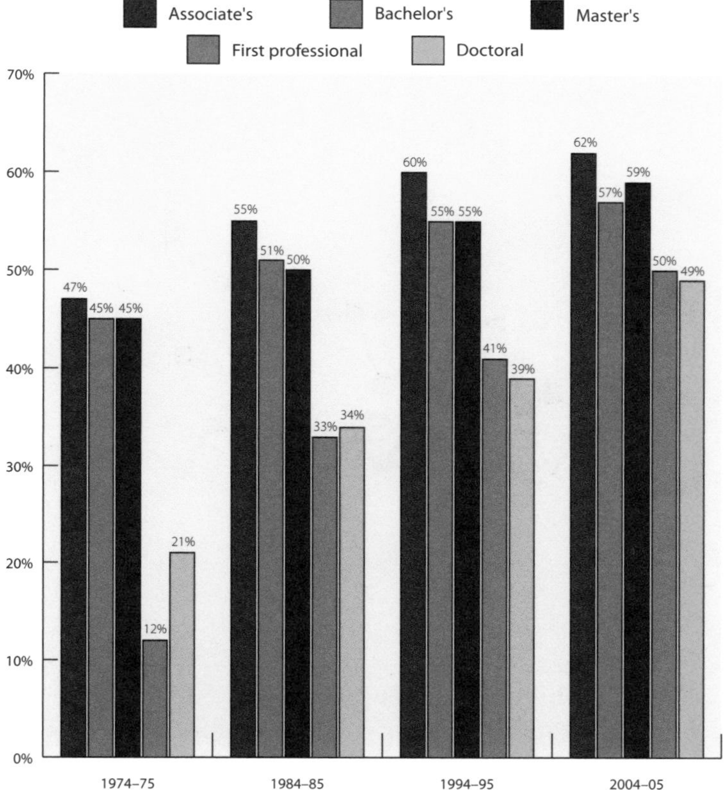

Source: U.S. Department of Education, National Center for Education Statistics, *Digest of Education Statistics 2006*, by Thomas D. Snyder, Sally A. Dillow, & Charlene M. Hoffman (NCES 2007-017). Washington, DC: U.S. Government Printing Office, 2007, Table 251.

in female and male earnings attributable to factors such as discrimination, preferences, and circumstances (Dougherty, 2005). All of these factors may contribute to the rising numbers of women earning college degrees.

Across races/ethnicities, women are more likely than men to earn a bachelor's degree. In 2003–04, women comprised 54 percent of Asian American, 56 percent of white, 59 percent of Hispanic, 63 percent of American Indian, and 64 percent of African American undergraduates (King, 2006). The gaps in college graduation are more pronounced by race/ethnicity than by gender. Among 25- to 29-year-olds in 2006, white women and men were much more likely to hold a bachelor's degree than were African American and His-

Figure 33. Percentage of 25- to 29-Year-Olds With a Bachelor's Degree or Higher, by Race/Ethnicity and Gender, 1971–2006

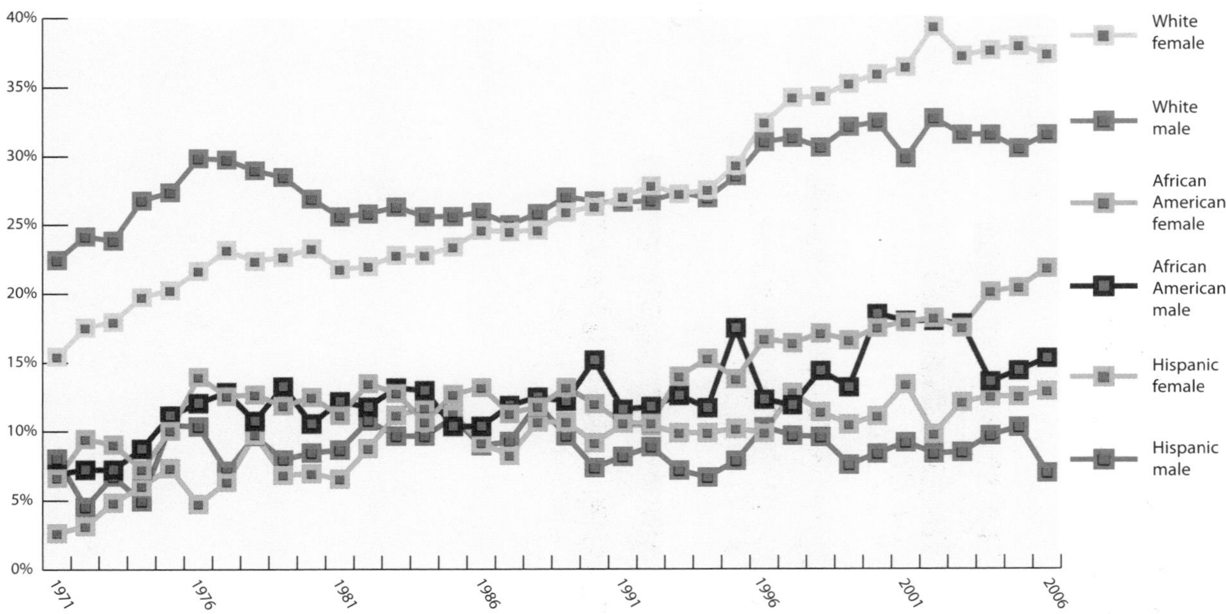

Source: U.S. Department of Education, National Center for Education Statistics, *The Condition of Education 2007* (NCES 2007-064). Washington, DC: Author, 2007

panic women and men. Among women, 37 percent of white women had earned a bachelor's or higher degree in 2006, compared with 22 percent of African American and only 13 percent of Hispanic women in the same age group. While gaps by race/ethnicity are evident, the percentage of 25- to 29-year-olds who have college degrees is generally increasing for every group except Hispanic men, who show no clear trend (Bacolod & Hotz, 2006) (see Figure 33). The *number* of Hispanic men earning college degrees, however, is increasing (see Figure 34).[23]

Other important factors in understanding trends among women and men attending college are age, income, and dependency status. For example, the gender gap in college attendance is almost absent among those entering college directly after graduating from high

---

[23] The population of Hispanic women and men in the United States is growing at a much faster rate than that of other groups. The U.S. Census Bureau estimates that between April 2000 and July 2006 alone, the Hispanic population in the United States increased by 25 percent. By comparison, the population of African Americans is estimated to have increased by 7 percent and the white population by 1 to 2 percent during the same period (U.S. Census Bureau, 2007; U.S. Census Bureau, Population Division, 2004).

Figure 34. Number of Bachelor's Degrees Conferred to African American and Hispanic Students, by Gender and Race/Ethnicity, 1977–2005

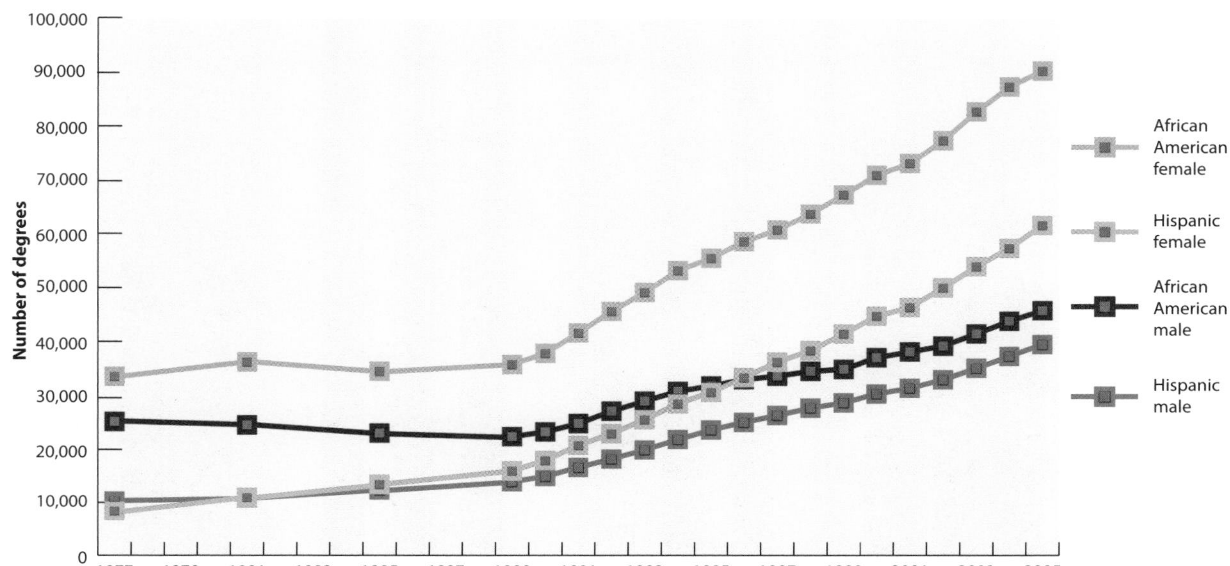

Source: U.S. Department of Education, National Center for Education Statistics, *Digest of Education Statistics 2006,* by Thomas D. Snyder, Sally A. Dillow, & Charlene M. Hoffman (NCES 2007-017). Washington, DC: U.S. Government Printing Office, 2007.

school. Of the 2.5 million students who graduated from high school between October 2005 and October 2006, 1.6 million (65.8 percent) were attending college in October 2006. The college enrollment rate of young women, 66.0 percent, was approximately the same as that of young men, 65.5 percent (U.S. Department of Labor, Bureau of Labor Statistics, 2007). Among traditional-age students (under age 24), the gender gap favoring women earning an undergraduate degree appears only among students from low- and middle-income families (King, 2006), and the gap is largest among students from low-income families (Goldin, Katz, & Kuziemko, 2006).

The economic situation of college students differs by dependency status (about half of undergraduates were dependent in 2003–04).[24] With regard to dependent students, as family income rises, the gen-

[24] Dependent students are defined for federal financial aid purposes as those who are 24 years of age or younger, single, childless, and not veterans or wards of the court. Independent students are defined as those who are age 25 or older or students who are younger than 25 and are married, have children, or are veterans or wards of the court.

Figure 35. Percentage of Dependent Undergraduates, by Gender, Race/Ethnicity, and Family Income Level, 2003–04

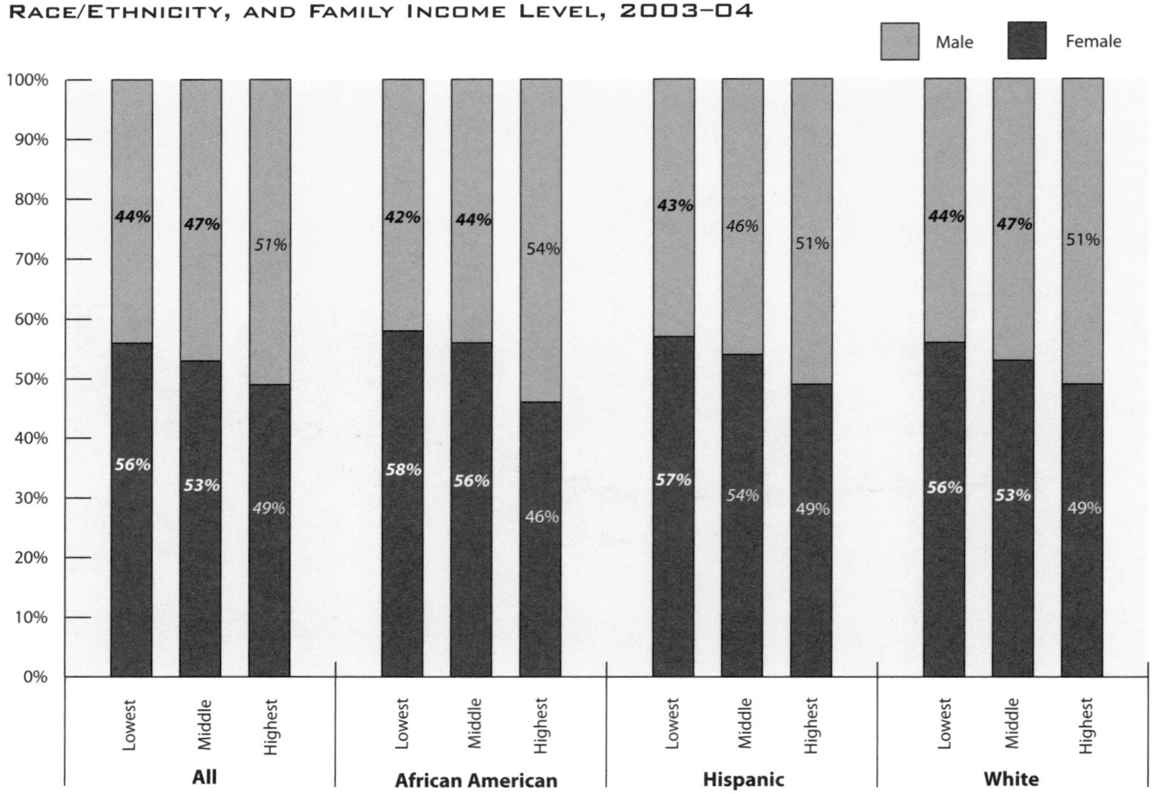

Note: Lowest quartile includes dependent students from families that earned less than $32,500 per year, middle 50 percent includes dependent students from families that earned $32,500 to $97,499 per year, and highest quartile includes dependent students from families that earned $97,500 or more per year. *Italic* indicates significant difference between genders within race/ethnicity and income level. **Bold** indicates significant difference from highest income level within gender within racial/ethnic grouping. Among Asian American students, no significant differences existed between genders at any income level or between proportions of female and male undergraduates by income level.

Source: King, Jacqueline, *Gender Equity in Higher Education: 2006*. Washington, DC: American Council on Education, 2006.

der gap favoring women diminishes to the point where it disappears (King, 2006). This pattern holds true across racial/ethnic groups (see Figure 35).

Among the 50 percent of undergraduates who are independent, the story is a bit different. While traditional-age women outnumber traditional-age men in college, larger disparities are found among older students, where women outnumber men by a ratio of almost 2-to-1. One-third of African American women who eventually graduate from college enroll when they are age 25 or older (ibid.). Unlike the situation described above for dependent students, women constitute a

Figure 36. Percentage of Independent Undergraduates, by Gender, Race/Ethnicity, and Family Income Level, 2003–04

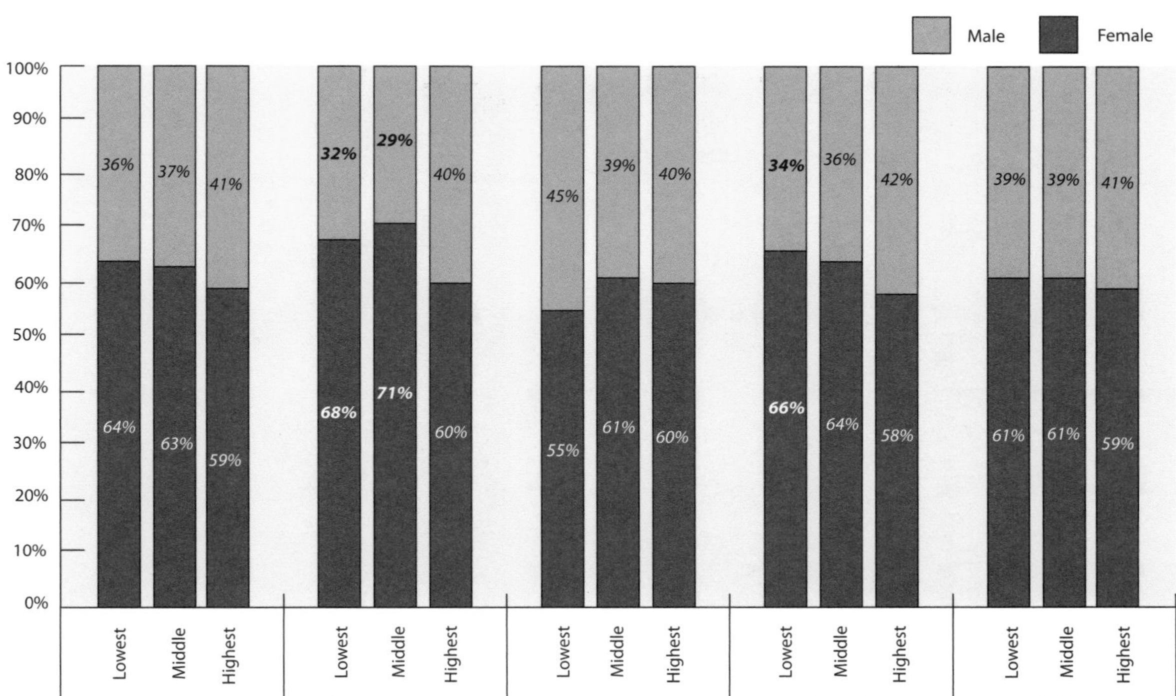

Note: Income quartiles vary by family size. For a family of two, the lowest quartile includes independent students from families that earned less than $11,020 per year, the middle 50 percent includes students from families that earned $11,020 to $42,627 per year, and the highest quartile includes students from families that earned $42,628 or more per year. *Italic* indicates significant difference between genders within race/ethnicity and income level. **Bold** indicates significant difference from highest income level within gender within racial/ethnic grouping.

Source: King, Jacqueline, *Gender Equity in Higher Education: 2006*. Washington, DC: American Council on Education, 2006.

majority of independent students among all racial/ethnic groups at all family income levels (see Figure 36).[25]

The number of female and male college graduates from all races/ethnicities has increased in recent decades. The proportion of degrees earned by minority men and women has, in general, gradually increased, while the share of degrees earned by white women and men has remained relatively constant and decreased, respectively. While the proportion of degrees earned by white men has decreased substantially from 49 percent to 33 percent since 1977,

[25] Despite this difference, for African American and Hispanic independent students, the percentage of women among students from lower-income families is greater than it is among students from higher-income families. This trend is not seen among other races/ethnicities. Overall and for Asian American and white independent undergraduates, the proportion of women does not vary by family income level.

Figure 37. Percentage of Bachelor's Degrees Conferred, by Gender and Race/Ethnicity, 1976–77 to 2004–05

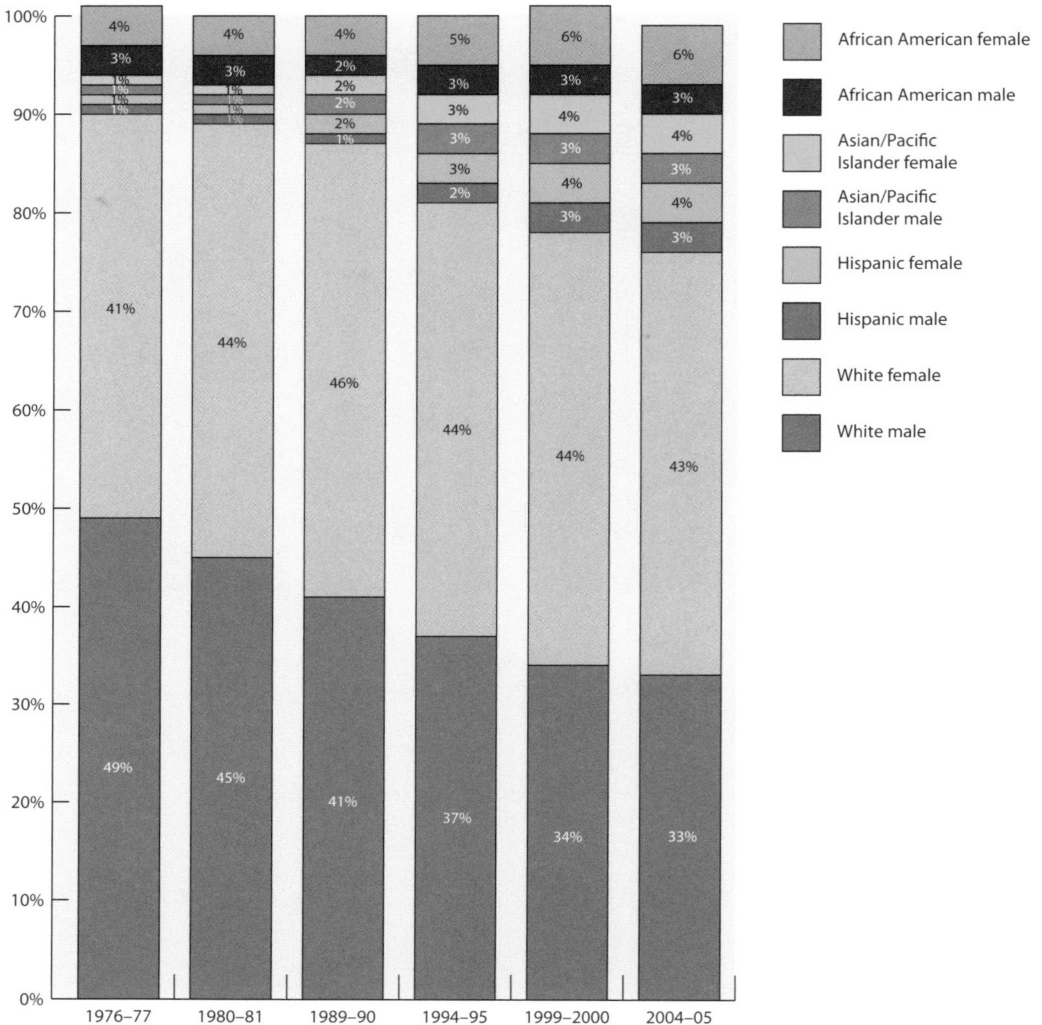

Source: U.S. Department of Education, National Center for Education Statistics, *Digest of Education Statistics 2006,* by Thomas D. Snyder, Sally A. Dillow, & Charlene M. Hoffman (NCES 2007-017). Washington, DC: U.S. Government Printing Office, 2007.

the number of white men earning bachelor's degrees has risen slightly, with white men earning approximately 438,000 bachelor's degrees in 1976–77 and 457,000 bachelor's degrees in 2004–05. African American men earned approximately the same percentage of degrees (3 percent) in 2004–05 as they did in 1976–77. In terms of actual numbers, however, 46,000 African American men earned degrees in 2004–05 compared to 25,000 in 1976–77 (U.S.

Figure 38. Percentage Distribution of General U.S. Population in 2006 and Bachelor's Degrees Conferred in 2005–06, by Gender and Race/Ethnicity

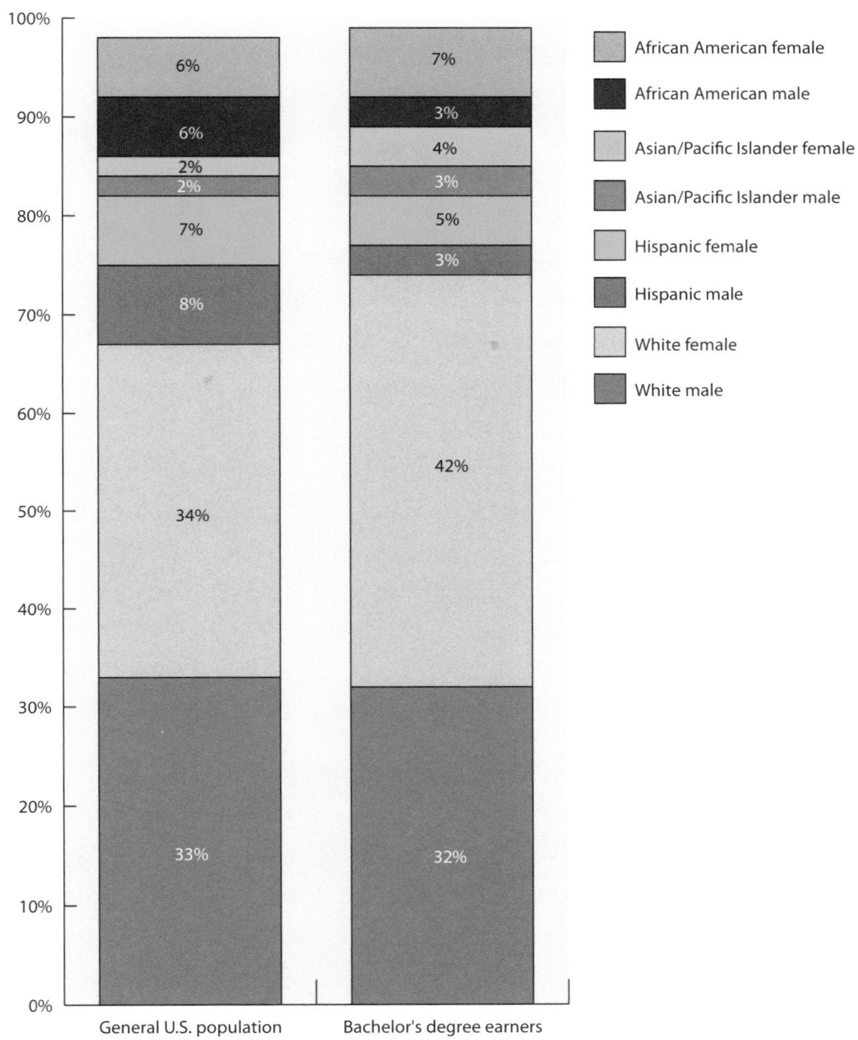

Note: Data include bachelor's degrees conferred by Title IV institutions, i.e., institutions that have a written agreement with the U.S. Secretary of Education that allows the institution to participate in any Title IV federal student financial assistance programs (other than the State Student Incentive Grant and the National Early Intervention Scholarship and Partnership programs). Degree earners data excludes nonresident aliens and students whose race/ethnicity was unknown.

Source: U.S. Census Bureau, Population Division. Table 3: Annual estimates of the population by sex, race, and Hispanic or Latino origin for the United States: April 1, 2000 to July 1, 2006 (NC-EST2006-03). Washington, DC: Author, 2007. U.S. Department of Education, National Center for Education Statistics, *Postsecondary Institutions in the United States: Fall 2006 and Degrees and Other Awards Conferred: 2005-06,* by Laura G. Knapp, Janice E. Kelly-Reid, Scott A. Ginder, & Elise Miller (NCES 2007-166). Washington, DC: Author, 2007.

Department of Education, National Center for Education Statistics, 2007b) (see Figure 37).

In part, the distribution of college degrees can be explained by the size of racial/ethnic groups in the general U.S. population. However, smaller percentages of African American men and Hispanic women and men earn degrees compared to their proportion of the general population (see Figure 38). In contrast, white and Asian American women are overrepresented in college compared to their respective percentages in the general population. White men and African American women earn bachelor's degrees in approximate proportion to their representation in the general population.

In summary, a gender gap favors women in college graduation, but women's gains have not come at men's expense. In all races/ethnicities, more women and men today than ever before are earning bachelor's degrees. Among traditional-age undergraduates from high-income families, more men than women attend college, and women outnumber men among older students and students from low- and middle-income families.

Where the Women Are in the Workplace

Perhaps the most compelling argument against a boys' crisis is that men continue to outearn women in the workplace. Among all women and men working full time, year round, women's median annual earnings were 77 percent of men's earnings in 2005 (Institute for Women's Policy Research, 2007). Looking at the college-educated, full-time work force one year out of college, women earned 80 percent of men's earnings on average in 2001, and 10 years out of college, women earned only 69 percent of men's earnings in 2003 (AAUW Educational Foundation, 2007). After controlling for factors known to affect earnings, such as education and training and demographic and personal choices including parenthood, a portion of these pay gaps remains unexplained (ibid.).

At various educational levels and within race/ethnicities, men consistently earn more than women earn (see Figure 39). Education

Figure 39. Median Earnings for Full-Time, Year-Round Workers Ages 25 and Older, by Race/Ethnicity, Educational Attainment, and Gender, 2005

Highest Level of Education	African American		Hispanic		White	
	Male	Female	Male	Female	Male	Female
Some high school but no high school degree	$23,597	$19,061	$25,334	$18,859	$31,049	$20,923
High school graduates (including GED holders)	$28,868	$24,001	$28,800	$23,283	$39,559	$27,389
Bachelor's degree	$46,017	$45,210	$49,472	$37,534	$61,486	$42,261

Source: U.S. Census Bureau, Current Population Survey, 2006 Annual Social and Economic (ASEC) Supplement. Washington, DC: Author, 2006.

is associated with higher earnings across the board, with some variation in the rate of increase. But overall it is clear that women's educational achievements have not yet fully translated into equity in the workplace.

Chapter 5

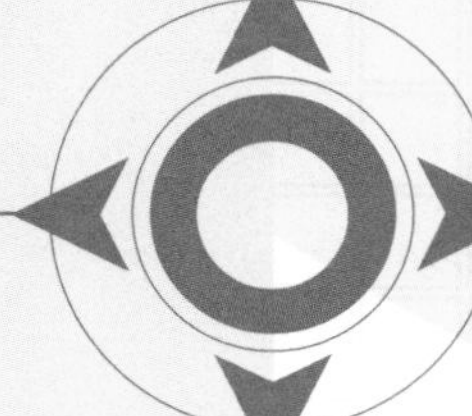

The True Crisis

The overarching message of this report is one of good news. Overall and within racial/ethnic groups and family income levels, girls and boys are improving by most measures of educational achievement, and most achievement gaps are narrowing. The past few decades have seen remarkable gains for girls and boys in education, and no evidence indicates a crisis for boys in particular. If a crisis exists, it is a crisis for African American and Hispanic students and students from lower-income families—both girls and boys.

The achievement gap by family income level is already apparent when children enter kindergarten (U.S. Department of Education, National Center for Education Statistics, 2007l). As students progress through the educational system, these achievement gaps remain stubbornly in place (Restuccia & Urrutia, 2004). On average, most children from families with higher incomes—both girls and boys—test well and go on to colleges and universities, whereas poor children perform poorly on tests and are more likely to enter the work force without a college degree (U.S. Department of Education, National Center for Education Statistics, 2006b). The achievement gap can also be observed between racial/ethnic groups, with African American and Hispanic students underperforming compared to their Asian American and white peers.

Exploring reasons for racial/ethnic disparities is beyond the scope of this report. It is important, however, to acknowledge the strong relationship between race/ethnicity and family income level. Researchers agree that part of the racial/ethnic differences in educational achievement results from differences in family income level, but the true extent of this overlap may be masked by limited measures of family income. For example, like many studies, this report uses eligibility for free or reduced-price school lunch as an indicator of family income level. Of course, large differences exist within the group of students whose family income exceeds the eligibility limit (more than $37,000 annually for a family of four in 2007). More precise definitions of income, such as those used in the SAT and ACT analysis in chapter 3, still do not account for wealth or family structure. A family in which both parents work and combine their income is typically in a different economic situation than is a family in which one parent is fully or partially out of the work force. Developing better measures of family economic well-being is one important tool for understanding the achievement gap by race/ethnicity. Other possible explanations for the educational achievement gaps by race/ethnicity include differences in school funding and quality, teacher expectations, and racism.

The U.S. student population has always been relatively diverse compared to other developed nations, and it is becoming more so. This trend makes understanding how educational achievement varies by race/ethnicity all the more important. In 2006, slightly more than half (58 percent) of U.S. schoolchildren were categorized as white, one-fifth (20 percent) as Hispanic, and 15 percent as African American. Asian American students and "other races" accounted for 4 percent each (U.S. Federal Interagency Forum on Child and Family Statistics, 2007). Because the growing diversity in schools will eventually lead to a more diverse labor force, the academic achievement of these racial/ethnic groups is important not only for individuals but also for the U.S. economy as a whole (Kao & Thompson, 2003; Roach, 2004).

This crisis is not a new phenomenon. The American educational system has always been deeply divided by race/ethnicity and family income level. The problem, however, is no less urgent simply because it is long-standing. These divisions among schoolchildren threaten America's fundamental principle of equal opportunity and demand our attention.

Appendix A

NAEP Supplementary Figures

Figure A1. Main NAEP Mathematics Assessment Proficiency, by Gender, Most Recent Year Assessed

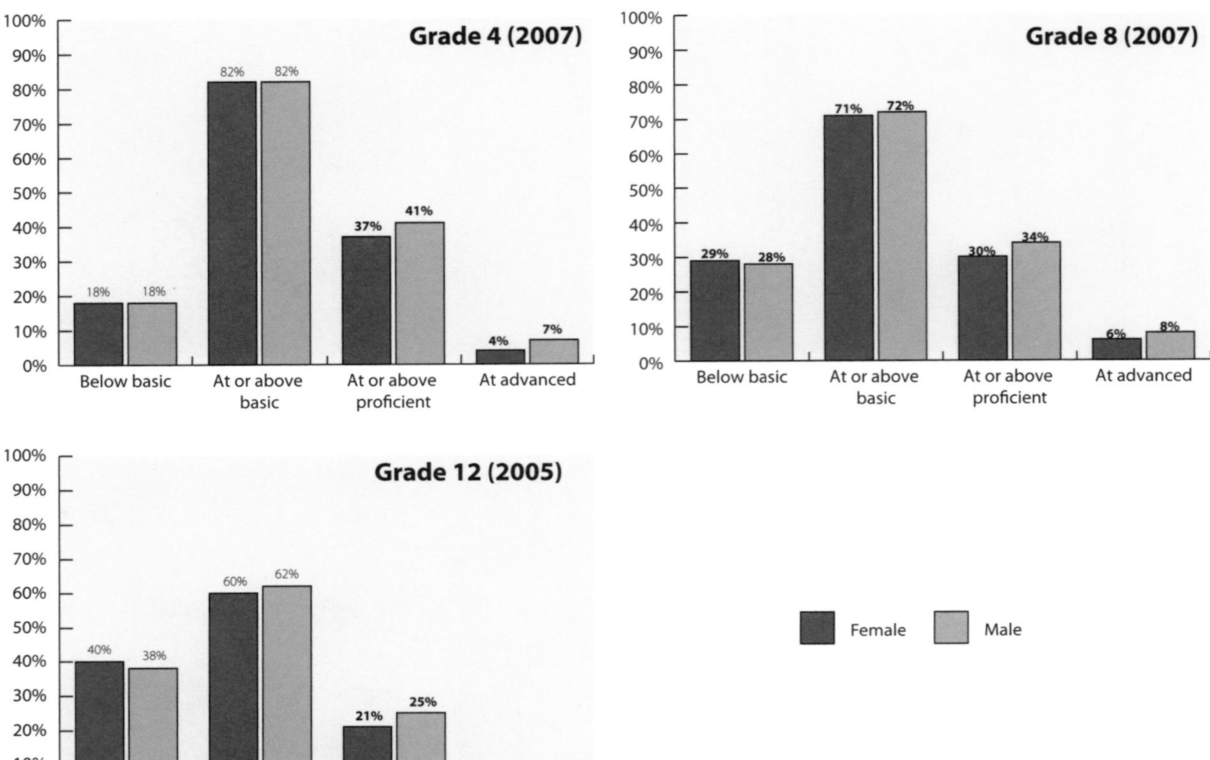

Note: **Bold** indicates significant differences between percentages of female and male test takers at a given proficiency level.

Source: U.S. Department of Education, National Center for Education Statistics, *NAEP Data Explorer*. Washington, DC: Author.

Figure A2. Main NAEP Mathematics Performance, by Proficiency Level and Gender, 1992–2007

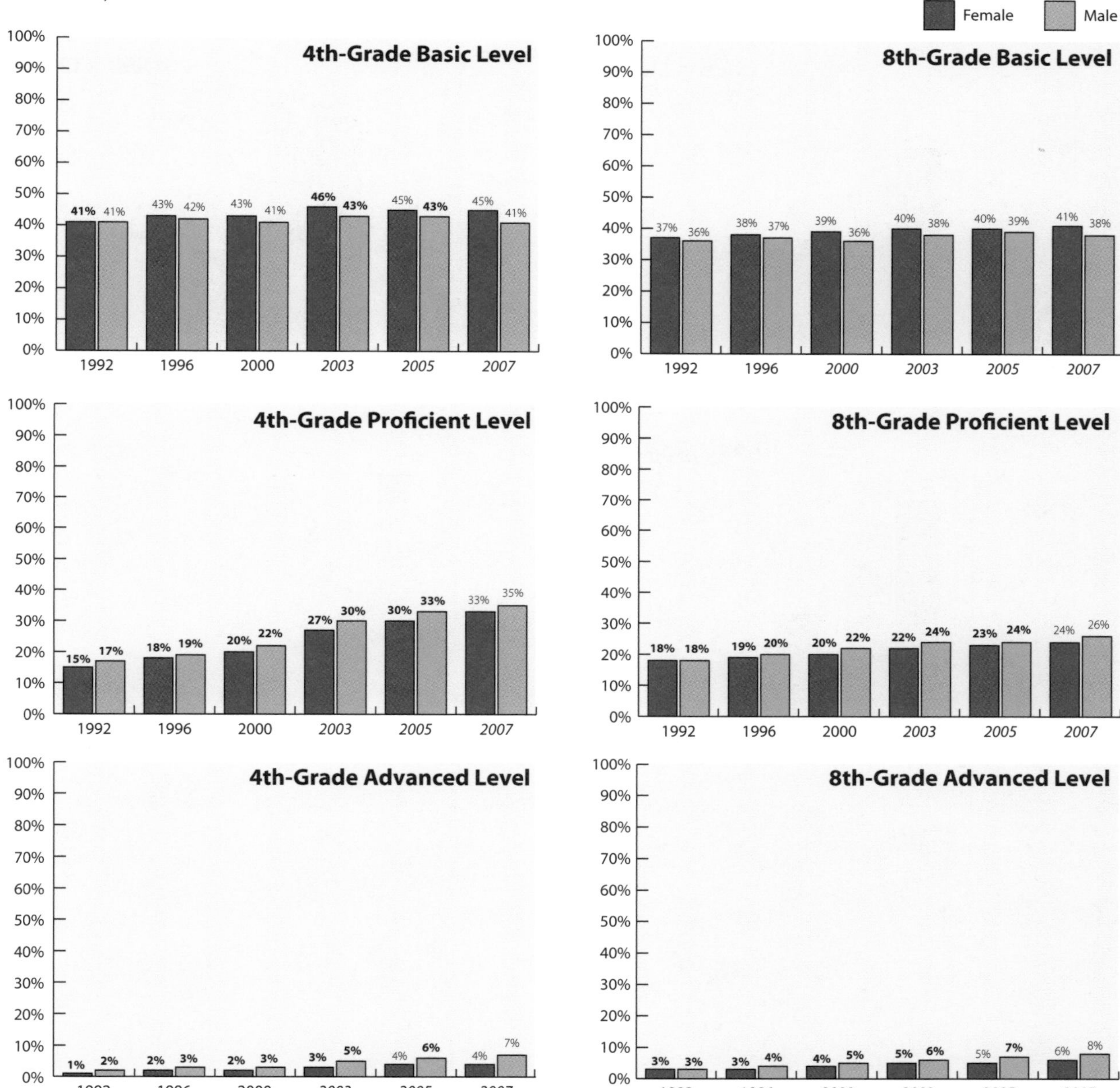

Note: Italic indicates year in which there were significant differences between percentages of female and male test takers at given level of proficiency. **Bold** indicates significantly different values from 2007. Because the 12th-grade math assessment changed significantly in 2005, charts showing proficiency levels by gender for 12th-grade students are not included. The eighth-grade math charts illustrate how the gender gap grows with proficiency. In 2007, more girls than boys performed at the basic level. Boys' advantage emerges at the next level of proficiency where 26.1 percent of boys and 24.3 percent of girls scored at the proficient level. At the same time, 8.1 percent of boys and 5.9 percent of girls scored at the advanced level. The difference between the percentage of girls and boys who scored at the proficient level is actually very close to the difference between the percentage of girls and boys who scored at the advanced level (1.8 percent vs. 2.2 percent). Because so many fewer students scored at the advanced level, however, the comparative gender gap is much greater at the advanced than at the proficient level. While only approximately 7 percent more boys than girls scored at the proficient level, approximately 37 percent more boys than girls scored at the advanced level.

Source: U.S. Department of Education, National Center for Education Statistics, *NAEP Data Explorer*. Washington, DC: Author.

Figure A3. Main NAEP Reading Assessment Proficiency, by Gender, Most Recent Year Assessed

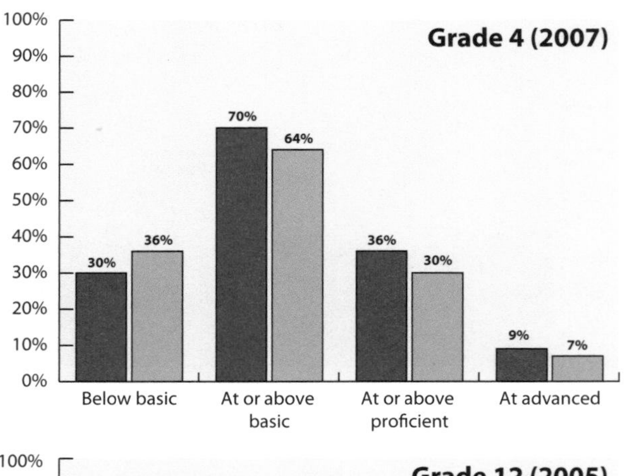

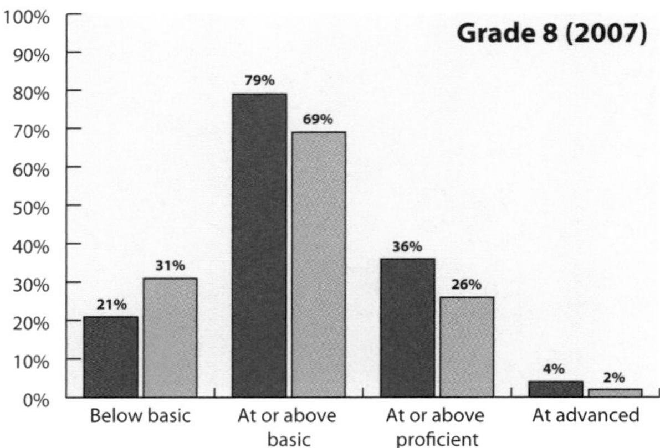

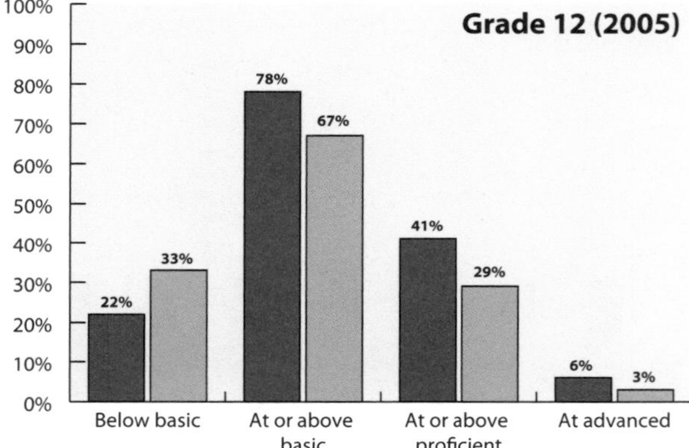

Note: **Bold** indicates significant differences between percentages of female and male test takers at a given proficiency level.

Source: U.S. Department of Education, National Center for Education Statistics, *NAEP Data Explorer*. Washington, DC: Author.

Figure A4. Main NAEP Reading Performance, by Proficiency Level and Gender, 1992–2007

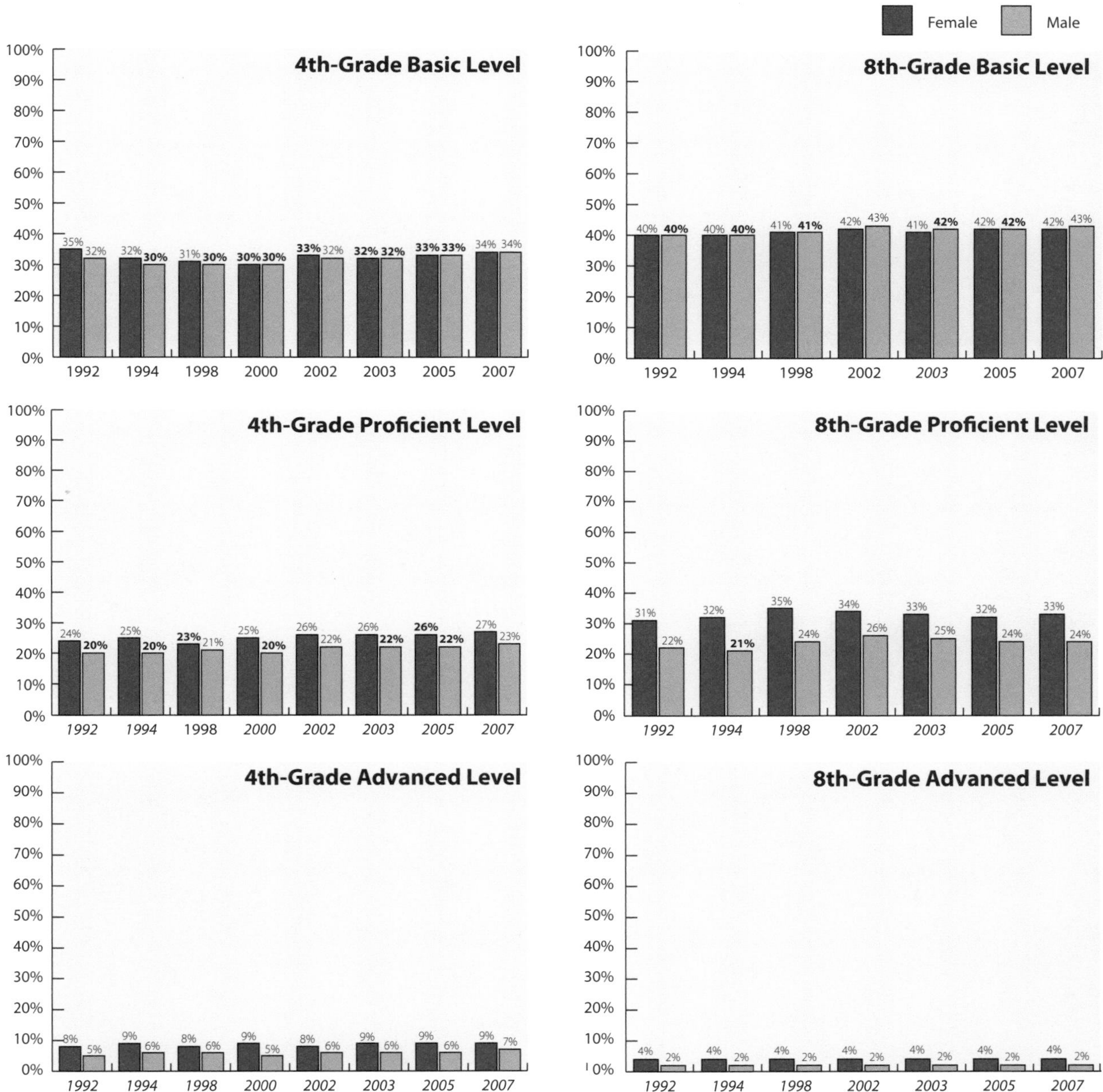

Note: Italic indicates years in which there were significant differences between percentages of female and male test takers at given level of proficiency. **Bold** indicates significantly different values from 2007.

Source: U.S. Department of Education, National Center for Education Statistics, *NAEP Data Explorer*. Washington, DC: Author.

Figure A5. NAEP-LTT Reading Assessment Average Scores, by Race/Ethnicity, 1975–2004

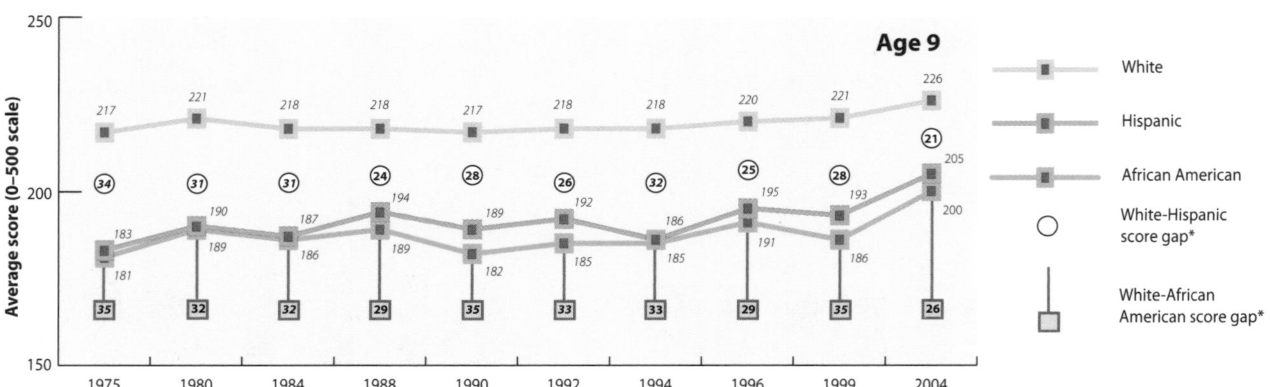

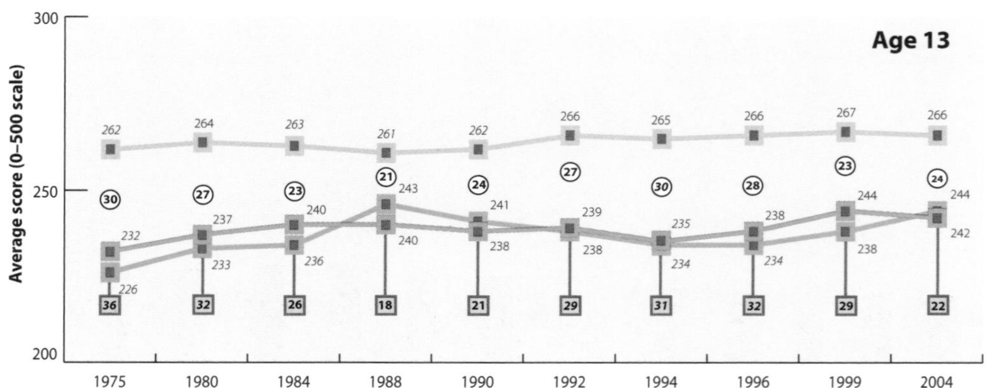

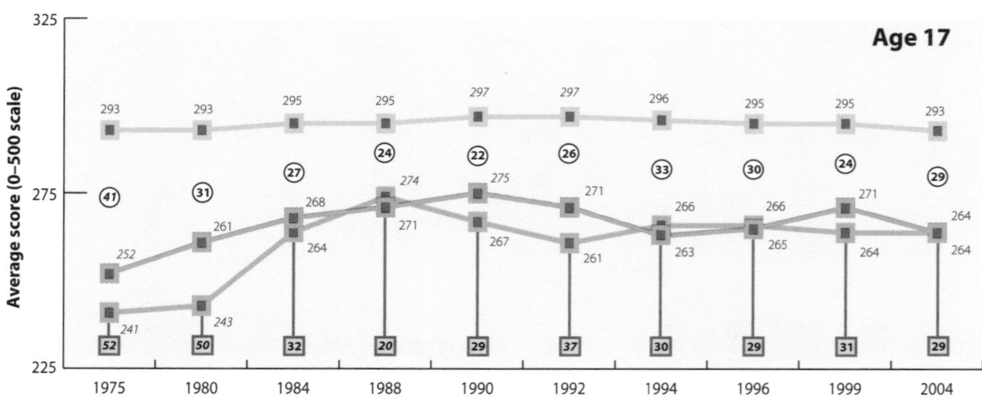

Note: Italic indicates significant difference from 2004. **Bold** indicates significant difference between racial/ethnic groups.

*White average score minus African American or Hispanic average score. Score gaps are calculated based on differences between unrounded average scores.

Source: U.S. Department of Education, National Center for Education Statistics, *NAEP Data Explorer*. Washington, DC: Author.

Figure A6. NAEP-LTT Mathematics Assessment Average Scores, by Race/Ethnicity, 1978–2004

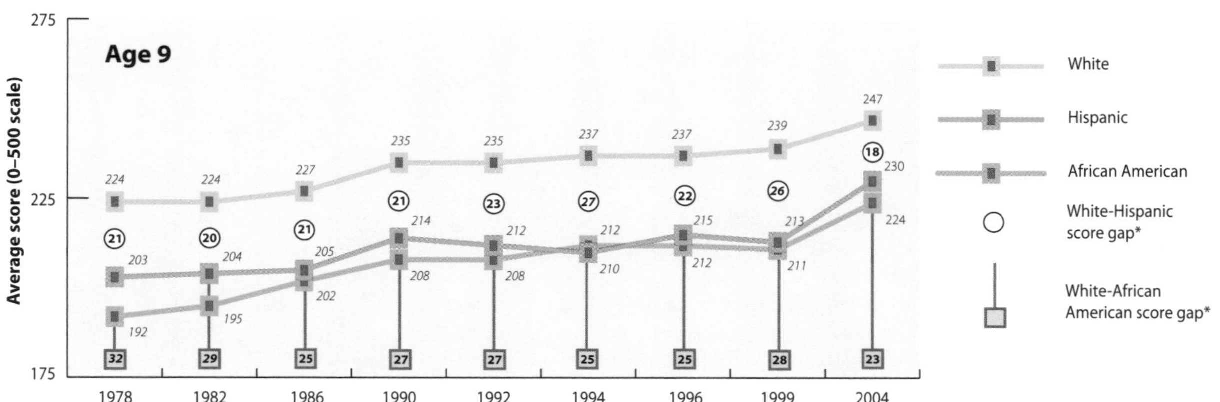

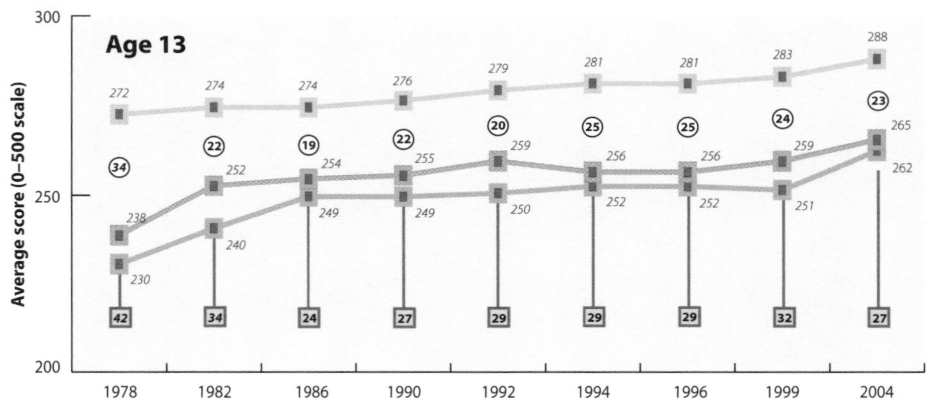

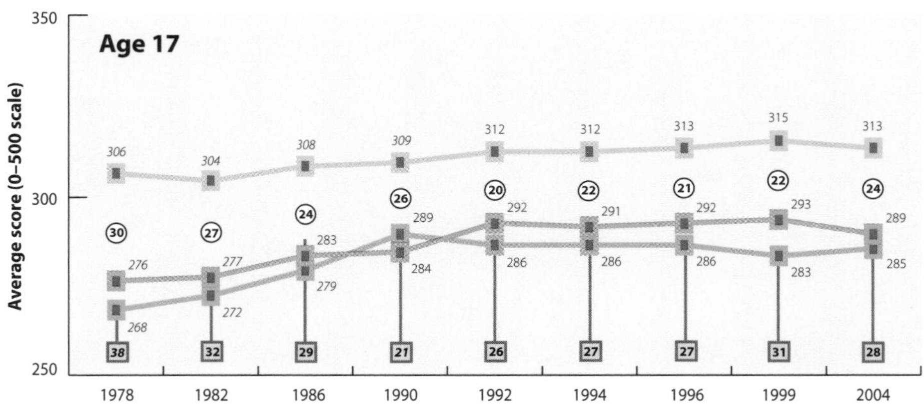

Note: Italic indicates significant difference from 2004. **Bold** indicates significant difference between racial/ethnic groups.

*White average score minus African American or Hispanic average score. Score gaps are calculated based on differences between unrounded average scores.

Source: U.S. Department of Education, National Center for Education Statistics, *NAEP Data Explorer*. Washington, DC: Author.

Figure A7. Main NAEP Mathematics Assessment Proficiency, by Race/Ethnicity, Most Recent Year Assessed

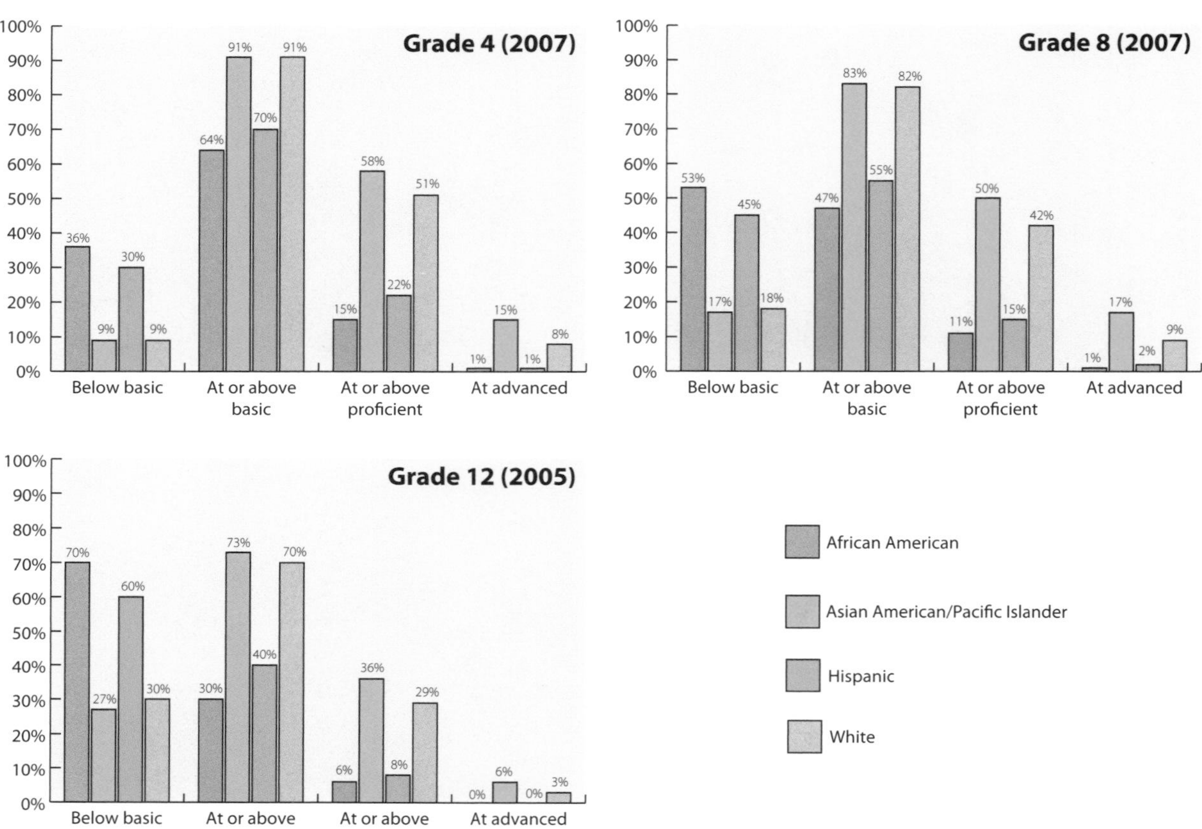

Source: U.S. Department of Education, National Center for Education Statistics, *NAEP Data Explorer*. Washington, DC: Author.

Figure A8. Main NAEP Reading Assessment Proficiency, by Race/Ethnicity, Most Recent Year Assessed

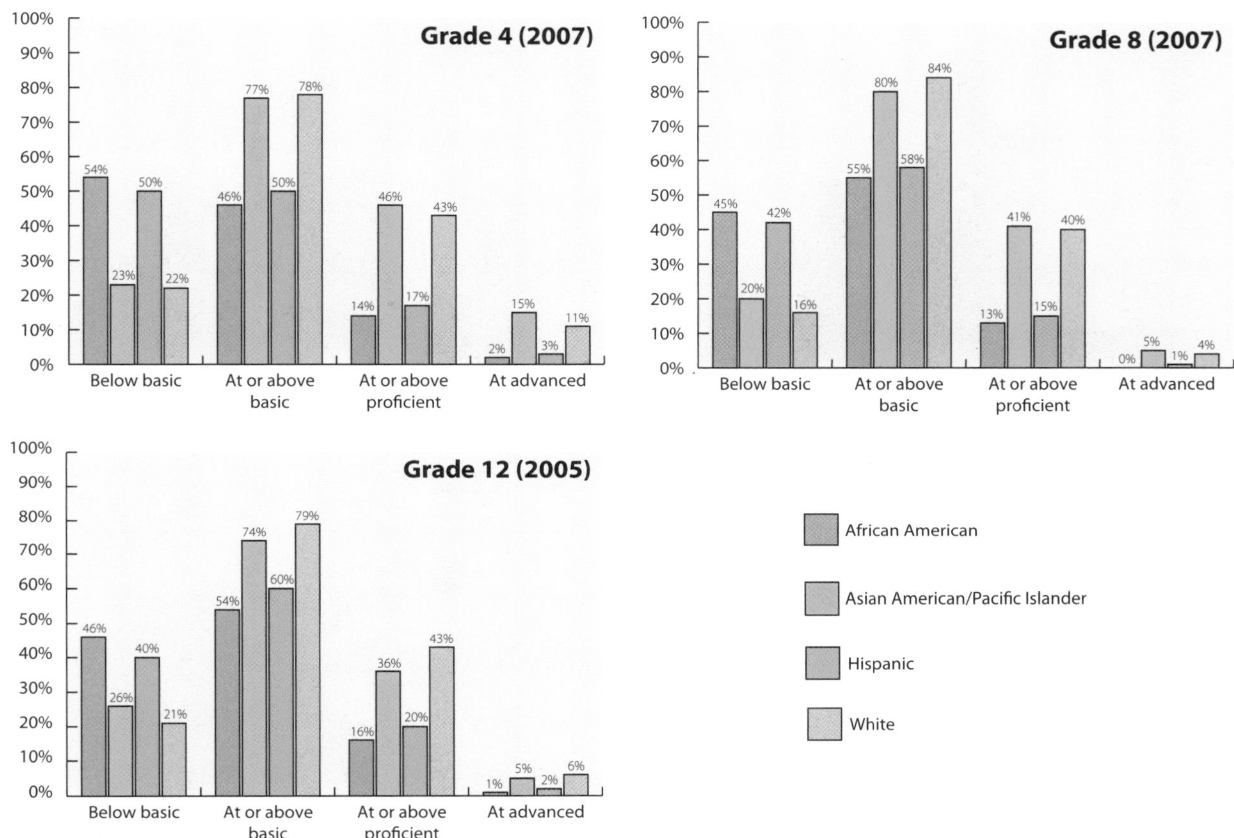

Source: U.S. Department of Education, National Center for Education Statistics, *NAEP Data Explorer*. Washington, DC: Author.

Figure A9. Main NAEP Mathematics Assessment Proficiency, by Family Income Level, Most Recent Year Assessed

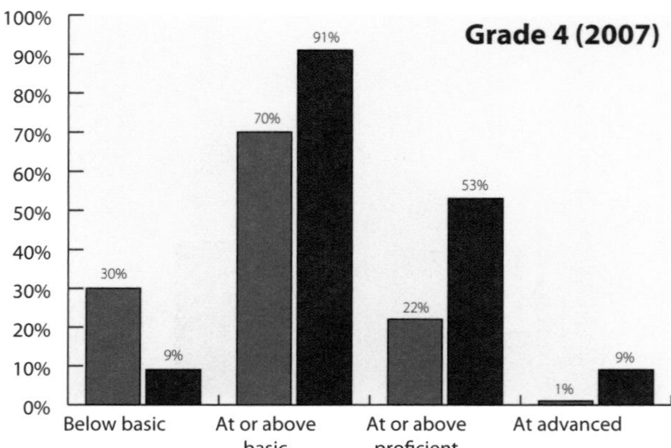

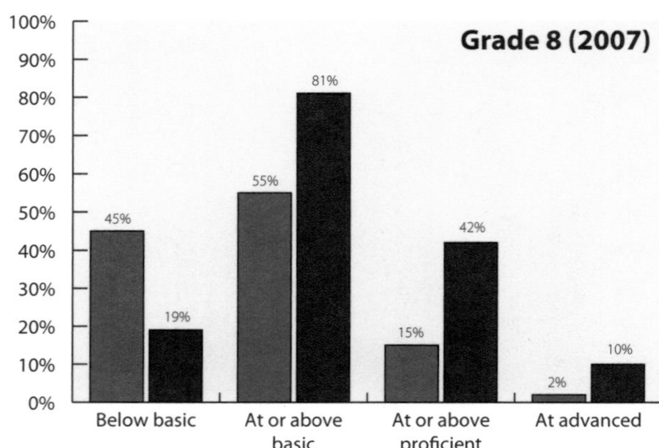

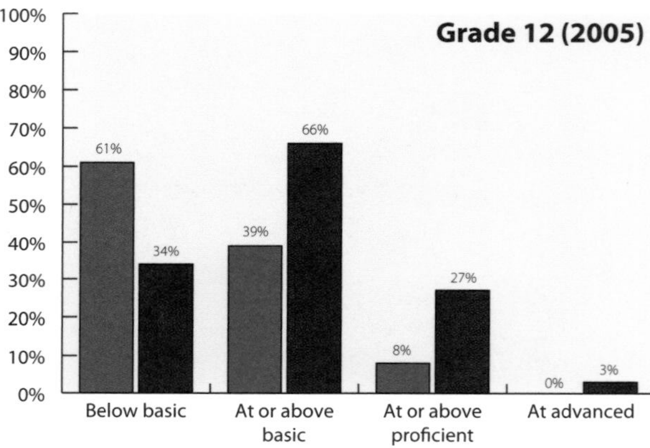

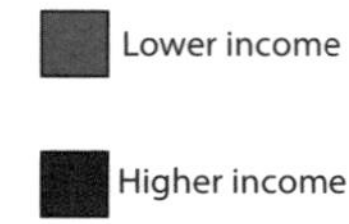

Note: Lower-income students are defined as those eligible for subsidized school lunch; higher-income students are defined as those not eligible. Differences are significant between percentages of lower-income and higher-income students at each level of proficiency.

Source: U.S. Department of Education, National Center for Education Statistics, *NAEP Data Explorer*. Washington, DC: Author.

FIGURE A10. MAIN NAEP READING ASSESSMENT PROFICIENCY, BY FAMILY INCOME LEVEL, MOST RECENT YEAR ASSESSED

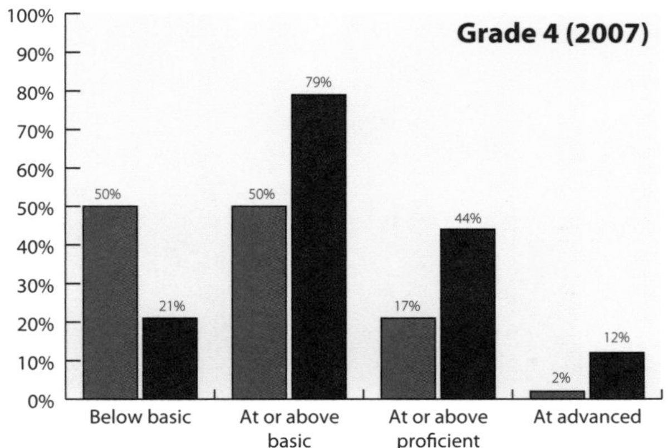

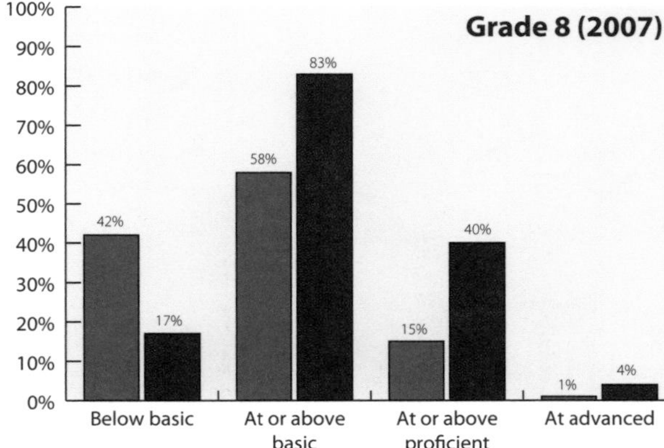

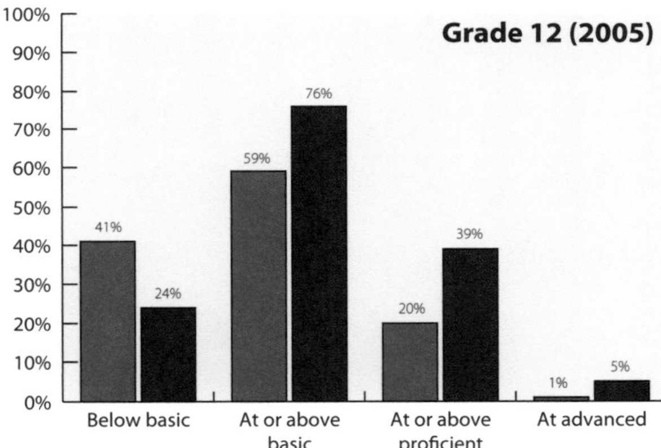

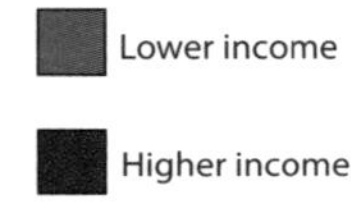

Note: Lower-income students are defined as those eligible for subsidized school lunch; higher-income students are defined as those not eligible. Differences are significant between percentages of lower-income and higher-income students at each level of proficiency.

Source: U.S. Department of Education, National Center for Education Statistics, *NAEP Data Explorer*. Washington, DC: Author.

Figure A11. Main NAEP Mathematics Assessment at or Above Basic Proficiency, by Race/Ethnicity and Gender, Most Recent Year Assessed

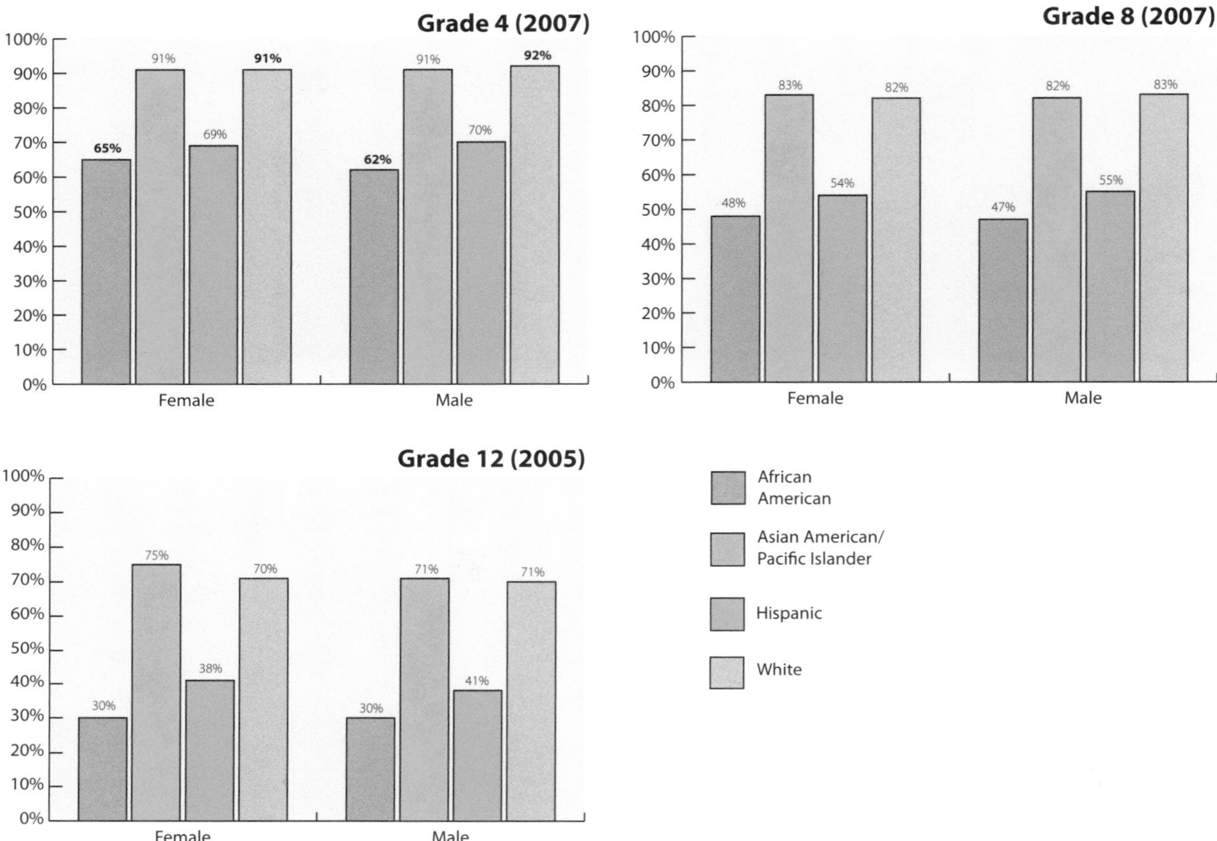

Note: **Bold** indicates racial/ethnic group in which there were significant differences between percentages of female and male test takers.

Source: U.S. Department of Education, National Center for Education Statistics, *NAEP Data Explorer*. Washington, DC: Author.

Figure A12. Main NAEP Reading Assessment at or Above Basic Proficiency, by Race/Ethnicity and Gender, Most Recent Year Assessed

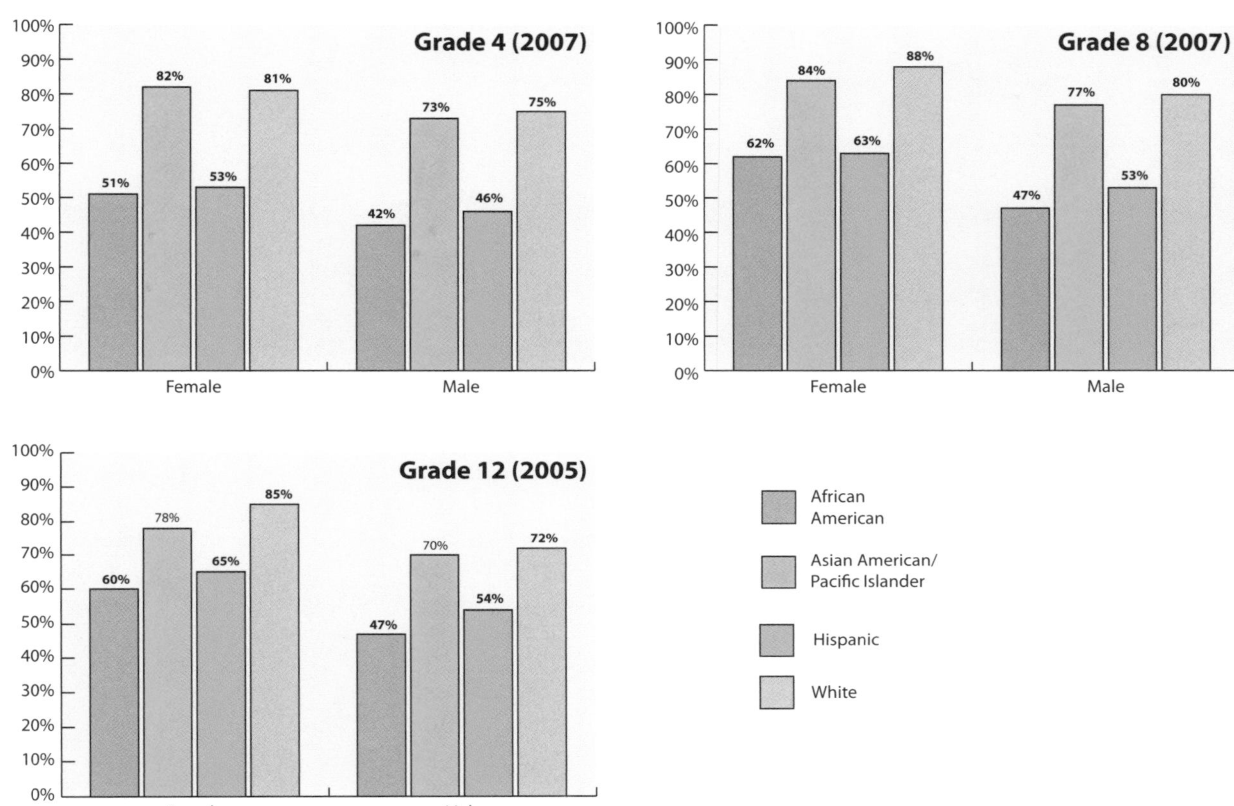

Note: **Bold** indicates racial/ethnic group in which there were significant differences between percentages of female and male test takers.

Source: U.S. Department of Education, National Center for Education Statistics, *NAEP Data Explorer*. Washington, DC: Author.

Appendix B

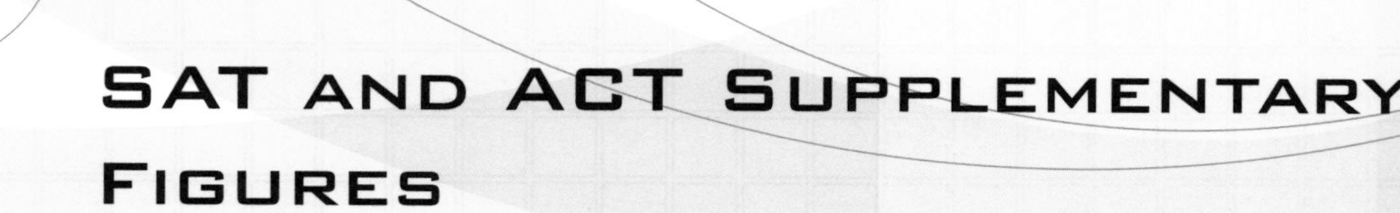

SAT and ACT Supplementary Figures

Figure B1. Percentage of High School Graduates Who Took the SAT or ACT, by State, 2001 and 2006

	SAT		ACT	
	2001	2006	2001	2006
Alabama	9	9	69	79
Alaska	51	51	34	25
Arizona	34	32	28	18
Arkansas	6	5	75	75
California	51	49	12	14
Colorado	31	26	62	100
Connecticut	82	84	4	12
Delaware	67	73	4	5
District of Columbia	56	78	26	30
Florida	54	65	40	45
Georgia	63	70	19	30
Hawaii	52	60	19	17
Idaho	17	19	59	57
Illinois	12	9	71	100
Indiana	60	62	20	20
Iowa	5	4	67	65
Kansas	9	8	78	75
Kentucky	12	11	72	76
Louisiana	7	6	80	74
Maine	69	73	6	10
Maryland	65	70	11	12
Massachusetts	79	85	8	13
Michigan	11	10	69	67
Minnesota	9	10	66	67
Mississippi	4	4	89	93
Missouri	8	7	70	70
Montana	23	28	55	57
Nebraska	8	7	74	76
Nevada	33	40	39	27
New Hampshire	72	82	7	12
New Jersey	81	82	4	8
New Mexico	13	13	64	60

	SAT		ACT	
	2001	2006	2001	2006
New York	77	88	14	17
North Carolina	65	71	13	14
North Dakota	4	4	80	80
Ohio	26	28	63	66
Oklahoma	8	7	71	72
Oregon	55	55	11	13
Pennsylvania	71	74	8	9
Rhode Island	71	69	5	8
South Carolina	57	62	28	39
South Dakota	4	4	70	75
Tennessee	13	15	79	93
Texas	53	52	33	29
Utah	5	7	69	69
Vermont	69	67	9	19
Virginia	68	73	10	15
Washington	53	54	17	15
West Virginia	18	20	61	64
Wisconsin	6	6	68	68
Wyoming	11	10	64	71

Source: Mary Beth Marklein, "All Four-Year U.S. Colleges Now Accept ACT Test," *USA Today,* March 18, 2007. Table based on data from the Western Interstate Commission for Higher Education, College Board, and ACT.

Figure B2. High School Graduates Who Took the SAT, by Gender and Race/Ethnicity, 1987 and 2007

	1987		2007	
	Number	Percent	Number	Percent
Gender				
Male	520,326	48%	690,500	46%
Female	560,100	52%	798,030	54%
Race/Ethnicity				
African American	88,037	8%	159,849	11%
Asian American	58,216	5%	140,794	9%
Hispanic	49,913	5%	168,544	11%
White	788,613	73%	828,038	55%

Source: College Board, *A Historical View of Subgroup Performance Differences on the SAT Reasoning Test,* by Jennifer L. Kobrin, Viji Sathy, & Emily J. Shaw (College Board Research Report No. 2006-5). New York: Author, 2007.

Figure B3. SAT Mean Verbal/Critical Reading Scores, by Gender, 1987–2006

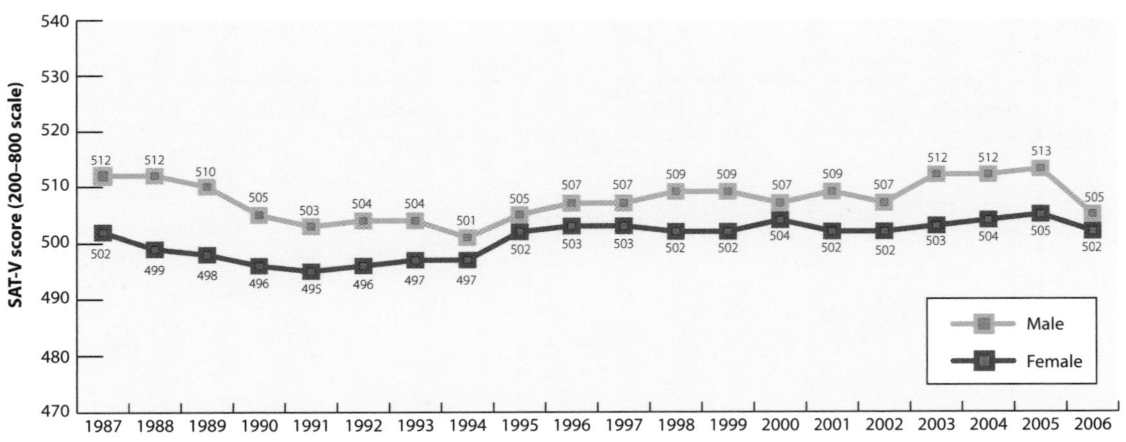

Note: Data based on total population of SAT takers.

Source: College Board, *A Historical View of Subgroup Performance Differences on the SAT Reasoning Test*, by Jennifer L. Kobrin, Viji Sathy, & Emily J. Shaw (College Board Research Report No. 2006-5). New York: Author, 2007.

FIGURE B4. SAT MEAN MATHEMATICS SCORES, BY GENDER, 1987–2006

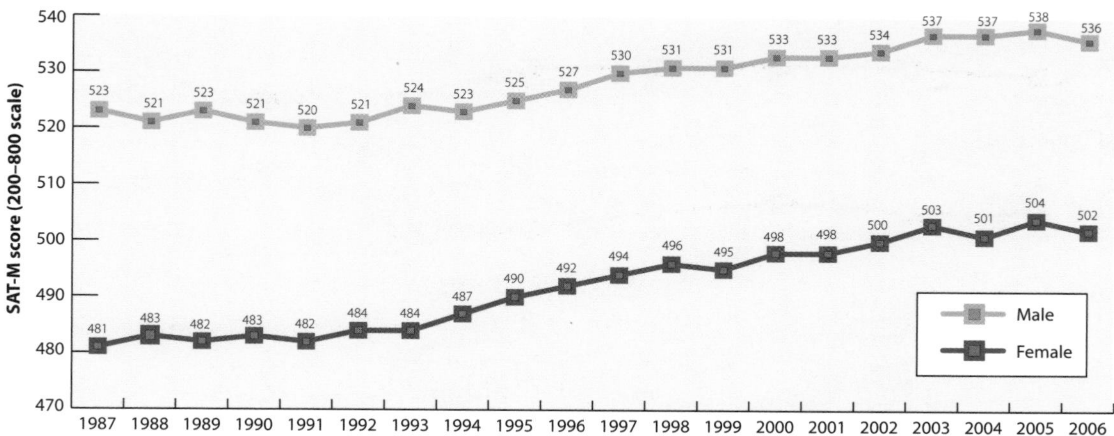

Note: Data based on total population of SAT takers.

Source: College Board, *A Historical View of Subgroup Performance Differences on the SAT Reasoning Test*, by Jennifer L. Kobrin, Viji Sathy, & Emily J. Shaw (College Board Research Report No. 2006-5). New York: Author, 2007.

FIGURE B5. SAT MEAN VERBAL/CRITICAL READING SCORES, BY GENDER AND FAMILY INCOME LEVEL, 1994–2004

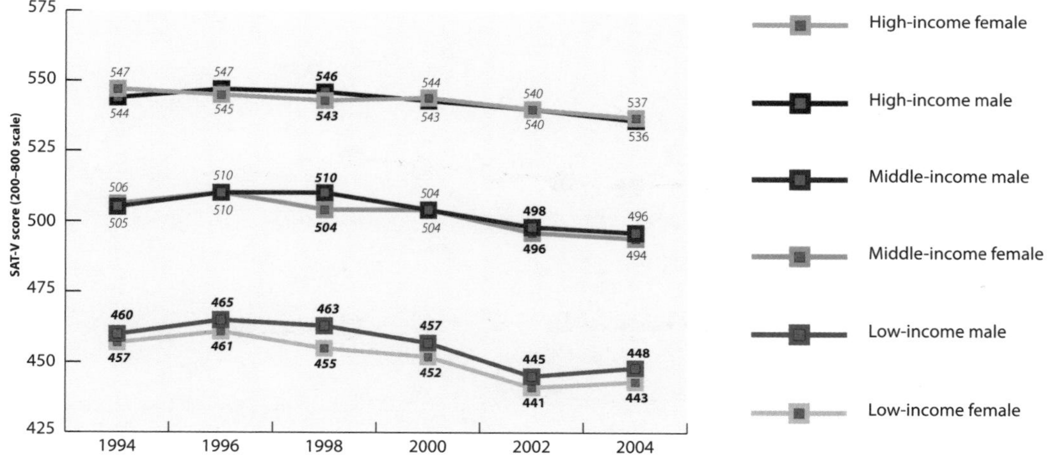

Note: Italic indicates a significant difference from 2004. **Bold** indicates a significant difference between female and male test takers of the same income group. Low-income students reported an annual family income of less than \$30,000, middle-income students reported an annual family income of \$30,000 to \$70,000, and high-income students reported an annual family income of more than \$70,000. Figures B5 and B6 show that performance for girls and boys from all income groups declined from 1994 to 2004 on both the SAT-M and SAT-V. This seems to be at odds with Figures 14 and 15, which show that performance has improved for both genders during this period. The discrepancy may be attributed to the composition of the sample. Between 1994 and 2004, a growing percentage of students did not report their family's income level. While 11 percent of the sample did not report income information in 1994, 31 percent did not report income information in 2004. Upon examination, nonresponders show a positive performance trend that counteracts the negative trend for responders. Additionally, income data is reported by \$5,000 to \$10,000 ranges and was not adjusted for inflation. Groups are not exactly equivalent across years.

Source: AAUW Educational Foundation analysis of unpublished data provided by the College Board.

Figure B6. SAT Mean Mathematics Scores, by Gender and Family Income Level, 1994–2004

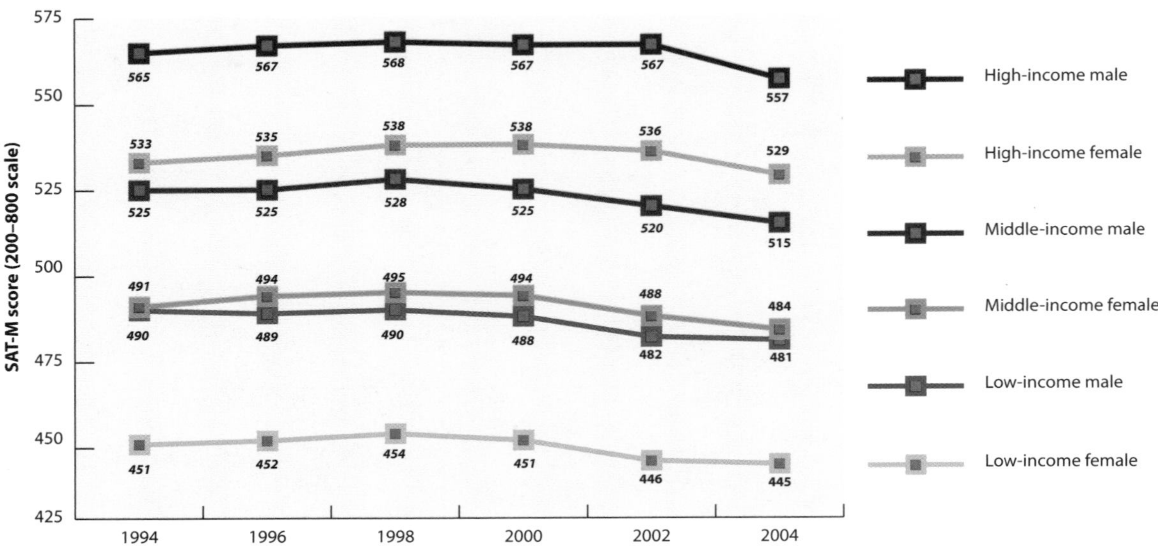

Note: Italic indicates a significant difference from 2004. **Bold** indicates a significant difference between female and male test takers of the same income group. Low-income students reported an annual family income of less than \$30,000, middle-income students reported an annual family income of \$30,000 to \$70,000, and high-income students reported an annual family income of more than \$70,000. See also note in Figure B5.

Source: AAUW Educational Foundation analysis of unpublished data provided by the College Board.

Figure B7. ACT Mean Mathematics Scores, by Gender and Family Income Level, 1997–2007

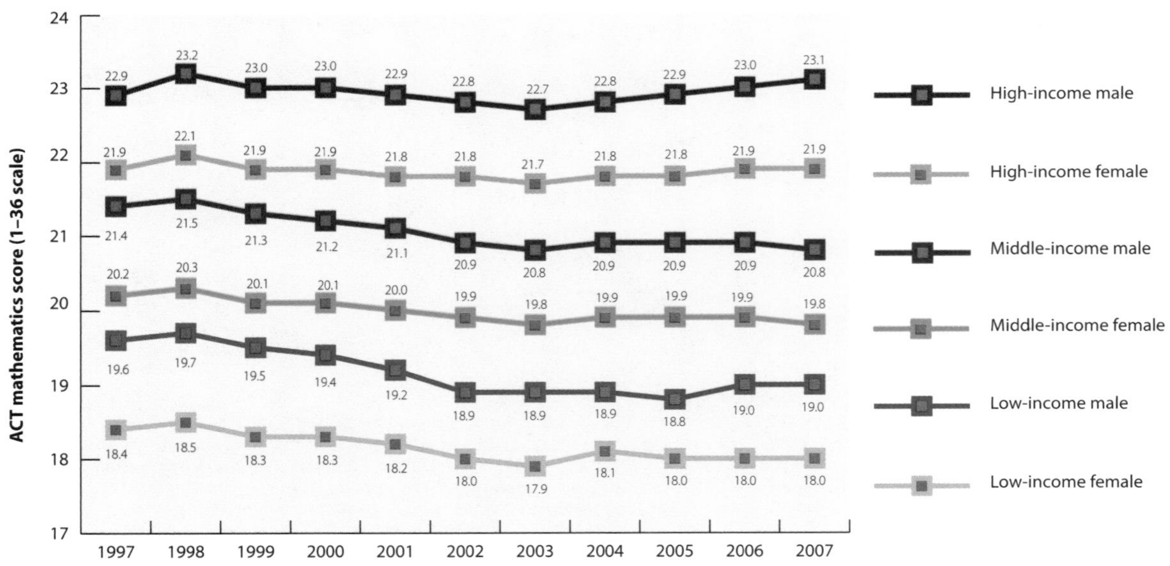

Note: Low-income students reported an annual family income of less than \$30,000, middle-income students reported an annual family income of \$30,000 to \$60,000, and high-income students reported an annual family income of more than \$60,000. Income figures not adjusted for inflation.

Source: Unpublished data provided to the AAUW Educational Foundation by the ACT Statistical Research Department.

Figure B8. ACT Mean English Scores, by Gender and Family Income Level, 1997–2007

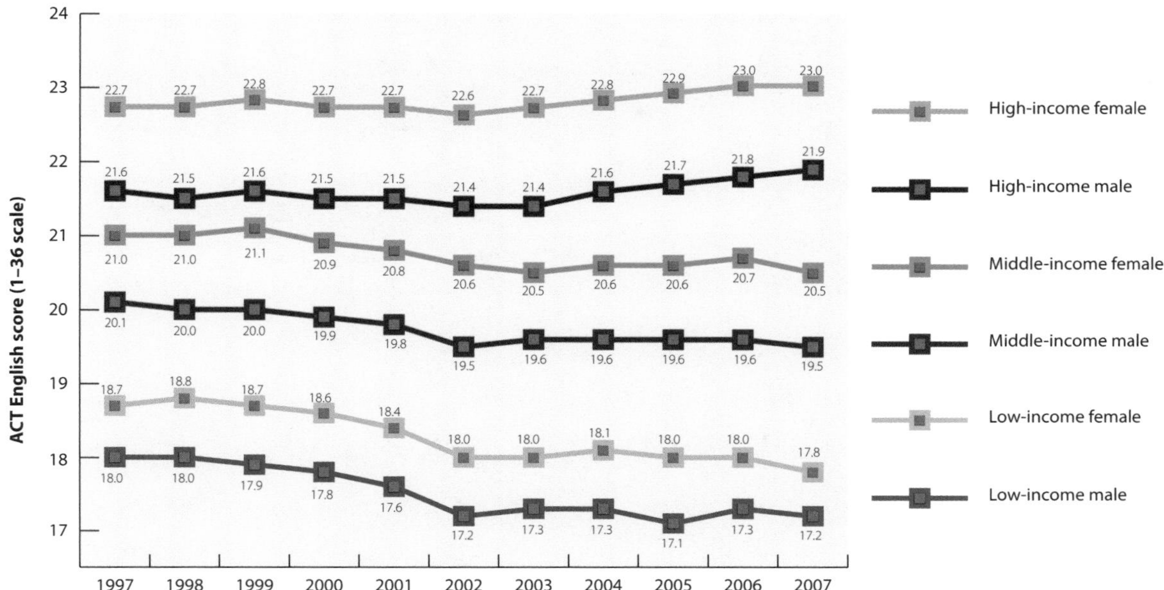

Note: Low-income students reported an annual family income of less than $30,000, middle-income students reported an annual family income of $30,000 to $60,000, and high-income students reported an annual family income of more than $60,000. Income figures not adjusted for inflation.

Source: Unpublished data provided to the AAUW Educational Foundation by the ACT Statistical Research Department.

Bibliography

AAUW Educational Foundation. (1992). *The AAUW report: How schools shortchange girls*. Washington, DC: Author.

————. (1996). *Girls in the middle: Working to succeed in school*. Washington, DC: Author.

————. (2001). *Beyond the "gender wars": A conversation about girls, boys, and education*. Washington, DC: Author.

————. (2007). *Behind the pay gap,* by Judy Goldberg Dey & Catherine Hill. Washington, DC: Author.

Academy for Education Development, Educational Equity Center. (2005). *Raising and educating healthy boys: A report on the growing crisis in boys' education*, by Merle Froschl & Barbara Sprung. New York: Author.

ACT Inc. (2005a). *ACT high school profile report: HS graduating class 2005: HS graduating class national report* (Code 990-000). Iowa City, IA: Author. Retrieved October 8, 2007, from http://www.act.org/news/data/05/pdf/data.pdf.

————. (2005b). *Gender fairness using the ACT* (Issues in College Readiness.) Iowa City, IA: Author. Retrieved July 10, 2007, from http://www.act.org/path/policy/pdf/gender.pdf.

————. (2006). *ACT high school profile report: The graduating class of 2006: National.* Iowa City, IA: Author. Retrieved October 8, 2007, from http://www.act.org/news/data/06/pdf/National2006.pdf.

————. (2007). *ACT high school profile report: The graduating class of 2007: National.* Iowa City, IA: Author. Retrieved October 8, 2007, from http://www.act.org/news/data/07/data.html.

Ainsworth, James W., & Vincent J. Roscigno. (2005). Stratification, school-work linkages, and vocational education. *Social Forces, 84*(1), 257–284.

Alaimo, Kara. (2005, March 15). New SAT could shrink test's gender gap. *Women's eNews.* Retrieved October 16, 2007, from http://www.womensenews.org/article.cfm/dyn/aid/2220.

Alexander, Karl L., Doris R. Entwisle, & Linda Steffel Olson. (2007, April). Lasting consequences of the summer learning gap. *American Sociological Review, 72*(2), 167–180. Retrieved October 16, 2007, from http://www.asanet.org/galleries/default-file/April07ASRFeature.pdf.

Allspach, Jill R., & Kelly Breining. (2005). *Gender differences and trends over time for the SAT reasoning test*. Princeton, NJ: Educational Testing Service.

Atkinson, Richard C. (2001, February 18). *Standardized tests and access to American universities*. Washington, DC: American Council on Education.

Bacolod, Marigee, & Joseph V. Hotz. (2006). Cohort changes in the transition from school to work: Evidence from three NLS surveys. *Economics of Education Review, 25*(4), 351–373.

Bickel, Robert, & A. Stan Maynard. (2004, January 28). Group and interaction effects with "No Child Left Behind": Gender and reading in a poor, Appalachian district. *Education Policy Analysis Archives, 12*(4). Retrieved May 15, 2006, from http://epaa.asu.edu/epaa/v12n4/.

Boone, William J., Steven R. Rogg, Jane Butler Kahle, & Arta Damnjanovic. (1997, March 22). *Race, gender, test length, and missing data: Why estimates of performance may be clouded.* Paper presented at the annual meeting of the National Association for Research in Science Teaching, Chicago, IL. (ERIC Document Reproduction Service No. ED406187).

Bracey, Gerald W. (2006, November). *Separate but superior? A review of issues and data bearing on single-sex education* (EPSL-0611-221-EPRU). Tempe, AZ: Education Policy Research Institute. Retrieved October 16, 2007, from http://epicpolicy.org/files/EPSL-0611-221-EPRU.pdf.

Bridgeman, Brent, & Cathy Wendler. (2005). *Characteristics of minority students who excel on the SAT and in the classroom* (Policy Information Report). Princeton, NJ: Educational Testing Service. Retrieved October 16, 2007, from http://www.ets.org/Media/Research/pdf/PICMINSAT.pdf.

Brown, Lyn Mikel, Meda Chesney-Lind, & Nan Stein. (2006). What about the boys? *Education Week, 25*(39), 35.

Campbell, Patricia B. (1989). So what do we do with the poor, non-white female? Issues of gender, race, and social class in mathematics and equity. *Peabody Journal of Education, 66*(2), 95–112.

Cech, Scott J. (2007). SAT scores take another dip. *Education Week, 27*(1).

Center on Education Policy. (2007, June). *Answering the question that matters most: Has student achievement increased since No Child Left Behind?* Washington, DC: Author.

Clotfelter, Charles T., Helen F. Ladd, & Jacob Vigdor. (2005). Who teaches whom? Race and the distribution of novice teachers. *Economics of Education Review, 24,* 377–392.

Cohen, Jacob. (1988). *Statistical power analysis for the behavioral sciences* (2nd ed.). Hillsdale, NJ: Lawrence Erlbaum Associates.

Coley, Richard J. (2001). *Differences in the gender gap: Comparisons across racial/ethnic groups in education and work.* Princeton, NJ: Educational Testing Service. (ERIC Document Reproduction Service No. ED451222). Retrieved October 16, 2007, from http://www.ets.org/Media/Research/pdf/PICGENDER.pdf.

College Board. (1988). *Sex differences in SAT scores,* by Nancy W. Burton, Charles Lewis, & Nancy Robertson (College Board Report No. 88-9). New York: Author.

————. (2006). *2006 college-bound seniors: State profile report: Maine.* Washington, DC: Author.

————. (2007a). *2007 college-bound seniors: State profile report: Maine.* Washington, DC: Author.

————. (2007b). *2007 college-bound seniors: Total group profile report.* Washington, DC: Author.

————. (2007c). *A historical view of subgroup performance differences on the SAT reasoning test*, by Jennifer L. Kobrin, Viji Sathy, & Emily J. Shaw (College Board Research Report No. 2006-5). New York: Author.

Datnow, Amanda, Lea Hubbard, & Elisabeth L. Woody. (2001). *Is single gender schooling viable in the public sector? Lessons from California's pilot program: Final report.* Toronto, Canada: Ontario Institute for Studies in Education. (ERIC Document Reproduction Service No. ED471051).

Dee, Thomas S. (2005, October). *Teachers and the gender gaps in student achievement* (NBER Working Paper No. 11660). Cambridge, MA: National Bureau of Economic Research.

DiPrete, Thomas A., & Claudia Buchmann. (2006, February). Gender-specific trends in the value of education and the emerging gender gap in college completion. *Demography, 43*(1), 1–24.

Dougherty, Christopher (2005). Why are the returns to schooling higher for women than for men? *The Journal of Human Resources, 40*(4), 969–988.

Dwyer, Carol A. (1976, May). Test content and sex differences in reading. *The Reading Teacher, 29*(8), 753–757.

Du, Yi, Christine M. Weymouth, & Kenneth Dragseth. (2003, April). *Gender differences and student learning.* Paper presented at the annual meeting of the American Educational Research Association, Chicago, IL.

Education Trust. (2006). *Education Watch 2006 state summary reports.* Washington, DC: Author. Retrieved October 4, 2007, from http://www2.edtrust.org/edtrust/summaries2006/states.html.

FairTest. (n.d.). *Gender bias in college admissions tests.* Retrieved September 8, 2007, from http://www.fairtest.org/facts/genderbias.htm.

Freer, Alexandra. (2003). *Girls' guide to the SAT: Tips and techniques for closing the gender gap.* New York: Princeton Review.

Geiser, Saul, & Roger Studley. (2001). *UC and the SAT: Predictive validity and differential impact of the SAT I and SAT II at the University of California.* Berkeley, CA: University of California, Office of the President. Retrieved October 17, 2007, from http://www.ucop.edu/sas/research/researchandplanning/pdf/sat_study.pdf.

Ginsberg, Alice E., Joan Poliner Shapiro, & Shirley P. Brown. (2004). *Gender in urban education: Strategies for student achievement.* Portsmouth, NH: Heinemann.

Girls Inc. (2006). *The supergirl dilemma: Girls grapple with the mounting pressure of expectations.* New York: Author.

Goldin, Claudia. (1992, June). *The meaning of college in the lives of American women: The past one-hundred years* (NBER Working Paper No. 4099). Cambridge, MA: National Bureau of Economic Research.

Goldin, Claudia, Lawrence F. Katz, & Ilyana Kuziemko. (2006, April). *The homecoming of American college women: The reversal of the college gender gap* (NBER Working Paper No. 12139). Cambridge, MA: National Bureau of Economic Research.

Graham, Kristen A., & Dan Hardy. (2006, April 2). In reading, Dick lags far behind Jane. *Philadelphia Inquirer.*

Greene, Jay P., & Marcus A. Winters. (2002, November). *Public school graduation rates in the United States* (Civic Report No. 31). New York: Manhattan Institute for Policy Research. Retrieved October 17, 2007, from http://www.manhattan-institute.org/pdf/cr_31.pdf.

————. (2005, February). *Public high school graduation and college-readiness rates: 1991–2002* (Education Working Paper 8). New York: Manhattan Institute for Policy Research. Retrieved October 17, 2007, from http://www.manhattan-institute.org/pdf/ewp_08.pdf.

————. (2006, April). *Leaving boys behind: Public high school graduation rates* (Civic Report No. 48). New York: Manhattan Institute for Policy Research. Retrieved October 17, 2007, from http://www.manhattan-institute.org/pdf/cr_48.pdf.

Gurian, Michael, & Kathy Stevens. (2005, May 2). What is happening with boys in school? *Teachers College Record.*

Hass, Nancy. (2006, November 5). Revisiting SAT essay: The writing section? Relax. *The New York Times,* Education Life Supplement Late Edition, Final, Section 4A, 14.

Hess, Frederick M., Andrew J. Rotherham, & Kate Walsh. (2005). *Finding the teachers we need* (Policy Perspectives). San Francisco: WestEd. Retrieved August 3, 2007, from http://www.wested.org/online_pubs/pp-05-01.pdf.

Institute for Women's Policy Research. (2007, April). *The gender wage ratio: Women's and men's earnings* (IWPR Fact Sheet #C350). Retrieved July 10, 2007, from http://www.iwpr.org/pdf/C350.pdf.

Jackson, Jerlando F. L., & James L. Moore III. (2006). African American males in education: Endangered or ignored? *Teachers College Record, 108*(2), 201–205.

Jones, Susanne M., & Kathryn Dindia. (2004). A meta-analytic perspective on sex equity in the classroom. *Review of Educational Research, 74*(4), 443–471.

Kanarek, Ellen A. (1988, October). *Gender differences in freshman performance and their relationship to use of the SAT in admissions.* Paper presented at the Northeast Association for Institutional Research Forum, Providence, RI.

Kao, Grace, & Jennifer S. Thompson. (2003). Racial and ethnic stratification in educational achievement and attainment. *Annual Review of Sociology, 29,* 417–442.

Karp, Stan. (2003). Some gaps count more than others. *Rethinking Schools, 18*(2).

Kessel, Cathy, & Marcia C. Linn. (1996). Grades or scores: Predicting future college mathematics performance. *Educational Measurement: Issues and Practice, 15*(4), 10–14.

Kimmel, Michael. (2006). A war against boys? *Dissent*, 65–70. Retrieved October 17, 2007, from http://dissentmagazine.org/article/?article=700.

King, Jacqueline. (2006). *Gender equity in higher education: 2006*. Washington, DC: American Council on Education.

Klecker, Beverly M. (2006). The "gender gap" in NAEP fourth-, eighth-, and twelfth-grade reading scores across years. *Reading Improvement, 43*(1), 50–56.

Klein, Joseph. (2004). Who is most responsible for gender differences in scholastic achievements: Pupils or teachers? *Educational Research, 46*(2), 183–193.

Klein, Susan S., Barbara Richardson, Dolores A. Grayson, Lynn H. Fox, Cheris Kramarae, Diane S. Pollard, & Carol Anne Dwyer (Eds.). (2007). *Handbook for achieving gender equity through education* (2nd ed.). Mahwah, NJ: Lawrence Erlbaum Associates.

Leonard, David K., & Jiming Jiang. (1999). Gender bias and the college predictions of the SATs: A cry of despair. *Research in Higher Education, 40*(4), 375–407.

Lewin, Tamar. (2006, July 9). At colleges, women are leaving men in the dust. *The New York Times*.

Lubienski, Sarah T. (2001, April). *A second look at mathematics achievement gaps: Intersections of race, class, and gender in NAEP data*. Paper presented at the annual meeting of the American Educational Research Association, Seattle, WA. (ERIC Document Reproduction Service No. ED454246).

Lubienski, Sarah T., Rebecca McGraw, & Marilyn Strutchens. (2004). NAEP findings regarding gender: Mathematics achievement, student affect, and learning practices. In Peter Kloosterman & Frank K. Lester Jr. (Eds.), *Results and interpretations of the 1990 through 2000 mathematics assessments of the National Assessment of Educational Progress* (pp. 305–336). Reston, VA: National Council of Teachers of Mathematics.

Marklein, Mary Beth. (2007, March 18). All four-year U.S. colleges now accept ACT test. *USA Today*. Retrieved December 18, 2007, from http://www.usatoday.com/news/education/2007-03-18-life-cover-acts_N.htm.

McGraw, Rebecca, Sarah Theule Lubienski, & Marilyn E. Strutchens. (2006). A closer look at gender in NAEP mathematics achievement and affect data: Intersections with achievement, race/ethnicity, and socioeconomic status. *Journal for Research in Mathematics Education, 37*(2), 129–150.

Mead, Sara. (2006, June). *The truth about boys and girls*. Washington, DC: Education Sector.

Mishel, Lawrence, & Joydeep Roy. (2006, April). *Rethinking high school graduation rates and trends*. Washington, DC: Economic Policy Institute.

National Governors Association. (2005). *Graduation counts: A report of the National Governors Association task force on state high school graduation data* (Redesigning the American High School). Washington, DC. Retrieved October 17, 2007, from http://www.nga.org/Files/pdf/0507grad.pdf.

Pappano, L. (2003, October 5). Girls seek to narrow gender gap on SAT. *The Boston Globe*.

Phillips, Gary W. (2007). *Linking NAEP achievement levels to TIMSS*. Washington, DC: American Institutes for Research. Retrieved October 17, 2007, from http://www.air.org/news/documents/naep-timss.pdf.

Pimentel, Allyson. (2004). *Supporting boys' resilience: A dialogue with researchers, practitioners, and the media*. New York: Ms. Foundation for Women. Retrieved October 17, 2007, from http://ms.foundation.org/user-assets/PDF/Program/supportingboys912.pdf.

Policy Analysis for California Education (PACE). (2004). *Voices from the field: Educators respond to accountability*, by Elisabeth L. Woody, Melissa Buttles, Judith Kafka, Sandra Park, & Jennifer Russell. Berkeley, CA: Author.

Porche, Michelle V., Stephanie J. Ross, & Catherine E. Snow. (2004). From preschool to middle-school: The role of masculinity in low-income urban adolescent boys' literacy skills and academic achievement. In Niobe Way & Judy Y. Chu (Eds.), *Adolescent boys: Exploring diverse cultures of boyhood*. New York: New York University Press.

Qian, Zhenchao, & Samuel H. Preston. (1993). Changes in American marriage, 1972 to 1987: Availability and forces of attraction by age and education. *American Sociological Review, 58*(4), 482–495.

Reed, Dianne, Lynn Fox, Mary Lou Andrews, Nancy Betz, Jan Perry Evenstad, Anthony Harris, et al. (2007). Gender equity in testing and assessment. In Susan S. Klein, Barbara Richardson, Dolores A. Grayson, Lynn H. Fox, Cheris Kramarae, Diane S. Pollard, & Carol Anne Dwyer (Eds.), *Handbook for achieving gender equity through education*. Mahwah, NJ: Lawrence Erlbaum Associates.

Reichert, Michael C., & Richard A. Hawley. (2006). Confronting the "boy problem": A self-study approach to deepen schools' moral stance. *Teachers College Record*.

Rennie Center for Education Research & Policy. (2006). *Are boys making the grade? Gender gaps in achievement and attainment*. Cambridge, MA: Author.

Restuccia, Diego, & Carlos Urrutia. (2004). Intergenerational persistence of earnings: The role of early and college education. *American Economic Review, 94*(5), 1354–1378.

Roach, Ronald. (2004). The great divide: Racial achievement gap gains recognition as national concern but solution continues to elude educators, scholars and policymakers. *Black Issues in Higher Education, 21*(1), 22.

Rosser, Phyllis. (1989). *The SAT gender gap: Identifying the causes.* Washington, DC: Center for Women Policy Studies. (ERIC Document Reproduction Service No. ED311087).

Rothstein, R. (1998). *The way we were? The myths and realities of America's student achievement.* New York: Century Foundation.

Sacchetti, Maria. (2006, December 25). Many forgoing SAT, path to college: In a fourth of schools, less than 60% take test. *The Boston Globe.* Retrieved June 10, 2007, from http://www.boston.com/news/local/articles/2006/12/25/many_forgoing_sat_path_to_college/.

Sadker, Myra, & David Sadker. (1994). *Failing at fairness: How our schools cheat girls.* New York: Touchstone.

Sharif v. New York State Education Department, No. 88 Civ. No. 8435 (S.D.N.Y. 1989).

Sommers, Christina Hoff. (2000). *The war against boys: How misguided feminism is harming our young men.* New York: Simon & Schuster.

Spencer, Renee, Michelle V. Porche, & Deborah L. Tolman. (2003). We've come a long way—maybe: New challenges for gender equity in education. *Teachers College Record, 105*(9), 1774–1807.

Strutchens, Marilyn. E., Sarah T. Lubienski, Rebecca McGraw, & Sarah K. Westbrook. (2004). NAEP findings regarding race and ethnicity: Students' performance, school experiences, attitudes and beliefs, and family influences. In Peter Kloosterman & Frank K. Lester Jr. (Eds.), *Results and interpretations of the 1990 through 2000 mathematics assessments of the National Assessment of Educational Progress* (pp. 269–304). Reston, VA: National Council of Teachers of Mathematics.

Thomas, June, & Cathy Stockton. (2003). Socioeconomic status, race, gender, & retention: Impact on student achievement. *Essays in Education*, 7. Retrieved October 18, 2007, from http://www.usca.edu/essays/vol7fall2003.html.

Tyre, Peg. (2006, January 30). The trouble with boys. *Newsweek.*

U.S. Census Bureau. (2006, August 29). *Current population survey, 2006 annual social and economic (ASEC) supplement.* Washington, DC: Author.

————. (2007). *Statistical abstract of the United States: 2007: School enrollment, faculty, graduates, and finances—projections 2005–2011.* Washington, DC: Author. Retrieved October 10, 2007, from http://www.census.gov/prod/2006pubs/07statab/educ.pdf.

U.S. Census Bureau, Population Division. (2004, October 1). *Resident population plus armed forces overseas—Estimates by age, sex, and race: July 1, 1971.* Washington, DC: Author. Retrieved October 16, 2007, from http://www.census.gov/popest/archives/pre-1980/PE-11-1971.xls.

————. (2007, May 17). Table 3: Annual estimates of the population by sex, race, and Hispanic or Latino origin for the United States: April 1, 2000 to July 1, 2006 (NC-EST2006-03). Washington, DC: Author. Retrieved June 6, 2007, from http://www.census.gov/popest/national/asrh/NC-EST2006/NC-EST2006-03.xls.

U.S. Department of Education, National Center for Education Statistics. (2001). *The Nation's Report Card: Mathematics 2000*, by J. S. Braswell, A. D. Lutkus, W. S. Grigg, S. L. Santapau, B. Tay-Lim, & M. Johnson (NCES 2001-517). Washington, DC: U.S. Government Printing Office.

———. (2002). *National education longitudinal study 1988: Fourth follow-up* (NELS:1988/2000). Washington, DC: Author. Data analysis system available from http://nces.ed.gov/dasolv2/tables/mainPage.asp?mode=NEW&filenumber=2.

———. (2004). *Trends in educational equity of girls & women: 2004*, by Catherine Freeman (NCES 2005-016). Washington, DC: U.S. Government Printing Office. Retrieved October 17, 2007, from http://nces.ed.gov/pubs2005/2005016.pdf.

———. (2005a). *NAEP 2004 trends in academic progress: Three decades of student performance in reading and mathematics*, by Marianne Perie, Rebecca Moran, & Anthony D. Lutkus (NCES 2005-464). Washington, DC: U.S. Government Printing Office. Retrieved October 17, 2007, from http://nces.ed.gov/nationsreportcard/pdf/main2005/2005464.pdf.

———. (2005b). *The Nation's Report Card long-term trend: Trends in average mathematics scale scores by gender.* Washington, DC: Author. Retrieved October 26, 2007, from http://nces.ed.gov/nationsreportcard/ltt/results2004/sub-math-gender.asp.

———. (2005c). *The Nation's Report Card long-term trend: Trends in average reading scale scores by gender*. Washington, DC: Author. Retrieved October 26, 2007, from http://nces.ed.gov/nationsreportcard/ltt/results2004/sub-reading-gender.asp.

———. (2005d). *The Nation's Report Card: Mathematics 2005*, by Marianne Perie, Wendy S. Grigg, & Gloria S. Dion (NCES 2006-453). Washington, DC: U.S. Government Printing Office. Retrieved October 17, 2007, from http://nces.ed.gov/nationsreportcard/pdf/main2005/2006453.pdf.

———. (2006a). *Dropout rates in the United States: 2002 and 2003*, by Jennifer Laird, Stephen Lew, Matthew DeBell, & Chris Chapman (NCES 2006-062). Washington, DC: Author. Retrieved October 17, 2007, from http://nces.ed.gov/pubs2006/2006062.pdf.

———. (2006b). *Placing college graduation rates in context: How 4-year college graduation rates vary with selectivity and the size of low-income enrollment*, by L. Horn (NCES 2007-161). Washington, DC: Author. Retrieved October 16, 2007, from http://nces.ed.gov/pubs2007/2007161.pdf.

———. (2007a). *The condition of education 2007* (NCES 2007-064). Washington, DC: Author. Retrieved October 18, 2007, from http://nces.ed.gov/pubs2007/2007064.pdf.

———. (2007b). *Digest of education statistics 2006*, by Thomas D. Snyder, Sally A. Dillow, & Charlene M. Hoffman (NCES 2007-017). Washington, DC: U.S. Government Printing Office. Retrieved October 18, 2007, from http://nces.ed.gov/pubs2007/2007017.pdf.

———. (2007c). *Mapping 2005 state proficiency standards onto the NAEP scales* (NCES 2007-482). Washington, DC: Author. Retrieved October 18, 2007, from http://nces.ed.gov/nationsreportcard/pdf/studies/2007482.pdf.

———. (2007d). NAEP data explorer. Washington, DC: Author. Data analysis system available from http://nces.ed.gov/nationsreportcard/naepdata.

———. (2007e). *The Nation's Report Card*. Washington, DC: Author. Retrieved October 16, 2007, from http://nces.ed.gov/nationsreportcard/.

———. (2007f). *The Nation's Report Card: America's high school graduates: Results from the 2005 NAEP high school transcript study*, by C. Shettle, S. Roey, J. Mordica, R. Perkins, C. Nord, J. Teodorovic, et al. (NCES 2007-467). Washington, DC: U.S. Government Printing Office. Retrieved October 18, 2007, from http://nces.ed.gov/nationsreportcard/pdf/studies/2007467.pdf.

———. (2007g). *The Nation's Report Card: Mathematics 2007*, by Jihyun Lee, Wendy S. Grigg, & Gloria S. Dion (NCES 2007–494). Washington, DC: Author. Retrieved October 17, 2007, from http://nces.ed.gov/nationsreportcard/pdf/main2007/2007494.pdf.

———. (2007h). *The Nation's Report Card: National Assessment of Educational Progress* website. Washington, DC: Author. Retrieved October 16, 2007, from http://nces.ed.gov/nationsreportcard/about/ltt_main_diff.asp.

———. (2007i). *The Nation's Report Card: Reading 2007*, by Jihyun Lee, Wendy S. Grigg, & Patricia L. Donahue (NCES 2007–496). Washington, DC: Author. Retrieved October 17, 2007, from http://nces.ed.gov/nationsreportcard/pdf/main2007/2007496.pdf.

———. (2007j). *The Nation's Report Card: 12th-grade reading and mathematics 2005*, by Wendy Grigg, Patricia L. Donahue, & Gloria Dion (NCES 2007-468). Washington, DC: Author. Retrieved October 17, 2007, from http://nces.ed.gov/nationsreportcard/pubs/main2005/2007468.asp#pdflist.

———. (2007k). *Postsecondary institutions in the United States: Fall 2006 and degrees and other awards conferred: 2005-06*, by Laura G. Knapp, Janice E. Kelly-Reid, Scott A. Ginder, & Elise Miller (NCES 2007-166). Washington, DC: Author. Retrieved October 17, 2007, from http://nces.ed.gov/pubs2007/2007166.pdf.

———. (2007l). *Preschool: First findings from the preschool follow-up of the early childhood longitudinal study, birth cohort (ECLS-B)*, by Jodi Jacobson Chernoff, Kristin Denton Flanagan, Cameron McPhee, & Jennifer Park (NCES 2008-025). Washington, DC: Author. Retrieved December 2, 2007, from http://nces.ed.gov/pubs2008/2008025.pdf.

———. (2007m). *Status and trends in the education of racial and ethnic minorities*, by Angelina KewalRamani, Lauren Gilbertson, Mary Ann Fox, & Stephen Provasnik (NCES 2007-039). Washington, DC: Author. Retrieved October 16, 2007, from http://nces.ed.gov/pubs2007/2007039.pdf.

U.S. Department of Labor, Bureau of Labor Statistics. (2007). *College enrollment and work activity of 2006 high school graduates* (USDL 07-0604). Washington, DC: Author. Retrieved October 18, 2007, from http://www.bls.gov/news.release/hsgec.nr0.htm.

U.S. Federal Interagency Forum on Child and Family Statistics. (2007). *America's children: Key national indicators of well-being 2007*. Washington, DC: Author. Retrieved October 16, 2007, from http://www.childstats.gov/pdf/ac2007/ac_07.pdf.

Viadero, Debra, & Robert C. Johnston. (2000). Lags in minority achievement defy traditional explanations. *Education Week, 19*(28), 1, 18–22. (ERIC Document Reproduction Service No. ED458335).

———. (2006). Concern over gender gaps shifting to boys. *Education Week, 25*(27), 1, 16–17. (ERIC Document Reproduction Service No. EJ738147).

Wainer, Howard, & Linda S. Steinberg. (1991). *Sex differences in performance on the mathematics section of the Scholastic Aptitude Test: A bidirectional validity study* (RR-91-45). Princeton, NJ: Educational Testing Service.

Weaver-Hightower, Marcus. (2005). Dare the school build a new education for boys? *Teachers College Record.*

West, Martha S., & John W. Curtis. (2006). *AAUP faculty gender equity indicators 2006*. Washington, DC: American Association of University Professors.

Willingham, Warren W., & Nancy S. Cole. (1997). *Gender and fair assessment.* Mahwah, NJ: Lawrence Erlbaum Associates.

Woody, Elisabeth L. (2002). Constructions of masculinity in California's single-gender academies. In Amanda Datnow & Lea Hubbard (Eds.), *Gender in policy and practice: Perspectives on single sex and coeducational schooling* (Sociology in Education). New York: RoutledgeFalmer.

Young, John W., & Jennifer L. Fisler. (2000). Sex differences on the SAT: An analysis of demographic and educational variables. *Research in Higher Education, 41*(3), 401–416.

Younger, Mike, & Molly Warrington. (2005). *Raising boys' achievement* (RR636). London, UK: Department for Education and Skills. Retrieved October 18, 2007, from http://www.dfes.gov.uk/research/data/uploadfiles/RR636.pdf.

Zwick, Rebecca. (2007). *College admission testing*. National Association of College Admission Counseling. Retrieved June 6, 2007, from http://www.nacacnet.org/NR/rdonlyres/21062AE7-F087-4CF8-A5BA-E5C3474F07C4/0/Standardized_Testing.pdf.

AAUW Equity Library

Behind the Pay Gap
AS60 ■ 54 pages/2007 ■ $10.00

Beyond the "Gender Wars": A Conversation About Girls, Boys, and Education
AS49 ■ 60 pages/2001 ■ $9.95

Drawing the Line: Sexual Harassment on Campus
AS58 ■ 58 pages/2005 ■ $12.00

Gaining a Foothold: Women's Transitions Through Work and College
AS37 ■ 100 pages/1999 ■ $6.49

Gains in Learning, Gaps in Earnings
2005 ■ www.aauw.org/research

Gender Gaps: Where Schools Still Fail Our Children
AS35 ■ Report ■ 150 pages/1998 ■ $6.99
AS36 ■ Executive Summary ■ 24 pages/1998 ■ $3.99

Girls in the Middle: Working to Succeed in School
AS29 ■ 128 pages/1996 ■ $7.49

Growing Smart: What's Working for Girls in School
AS26 ■ Report ■ 97 pages/1995 ■ $14.50
AS25 ■ Summary/Action Guide ■ 48 pages/1995 ■ $6.49

Hostile Hallways: Bullying, Teasing, and Sexual Harassment in School (2001)
AS50 ■ 56 pages/2001 ■ $9.95

Hostile Hallways: The AAUW Survey on Sexual Harassment in America's Schools (1993)
AS17 ■ 28 pages/1993 ■ $5.99

How Schools Shortchange Girls: The AAUW Report
AS22 ■ Report ■ 224 pages/Marlowe, 1995 ■ $6.49
AS14 ■ Executive Summary ■ 8 pages/1992 ■ $2.50

A License for Bias: Sex Discrimination, Schools, and Title IX
AS48 ■ 84 pages/AAUW Legal Advocacy Fund, 2000 ■ $12.95

SchoolGirls: Young Women, Self-Esteem, and the Confidence Gap
AS27 ■ 384 pages/Doubleday, 1994 ■ $12.95

Separated by Sex: A Critical Look at Single-Sex Education for Girls
AS34 ■ 99 pages/1998 ■ $12.95

Shortchanging Girls, Shortchanging America Executive Summary
AS20 ■ 20 pages/AAUW, 1994 ■ $5.99

¡Sí, Se Puede! Yes, We Can: Latinas in School
AS46 (English) ■ 84 pages/2001 ■ $12.95
AS47 (Spanish) ■ 90 pages/2001 ■ $12.95

Tech-Savvy: Educating Girls in the New Computer Age
AS45 ■ 84 pages/2000 ■ $12.95

Tenure Denied: Cases of Sex Discrimination in Academia
EF003 ■ 105 pages/2004 ■ $10.00

The Third Shift: Women Learning Online
AS51 ■ 80 pages/2001 ■ $9.95

Under the Microscope: A Decade of Gender Equity Projects in the Sciences
EF002 ■ 40 pages/2004 ■ $12.00

Voices of a Generation: Teenage Girls on Sex, School, and Self
AS39 ■ 95 pages/1999 ■ $7.50

Where the Girls Are: The Facts About Gender Equity in Education
AS61 ■ 103 pages/2008 ■ $12.00

Women at Work
AS55 ■ Report ■ 56 pages/2003 ■ $15.95
AS56 ■ Action Guide ■ 20 pages/2003 ■ $6.95
AS57 ■ Set (Report and Action Guide) ■ $19.95

To order reports, **call 800/225-9998** or visit **www.aauw.org**

❑ # Yes! I want to join AAUW's powerful network ...

Join online at www.aauw.org or use this form.

So I can take advantage of

- AAUW's scholarly research
- Opportunities for activism
- Tools to become an equity advocate
- Leadership training
- Professional and educational development opportunities

And so together we can

- Work to advance equity for women and girls through advocacy, education, and research
- Take grassroots activism to new levels
- Strengthen our collective voice in government
- Improve the lives of women and girls

AAUW Member

Membership is open to anyone holding an associate's or equivalent, bachelor's, or higher degree from a regionally accredited college or university.

Join today! Support AAUW initiatives at the national level by joining as a member-at-large. Member-at-large dues are $49 through June 30, 2008. After that date, call 800/326-AAUW (2289) for dues rates.

To become a branch member, join at the local level. Visit www.aauw.org or contact the AAUW Helpline at helpline@aauw.org or 800/326-AAUW (2289) to locate a branch in your area.

AAUW Student Affiliate

Student affiliates must be enrolled as undergraduates in a two- or four-year regionally accredited educational institution. Annual fees for student affiliate members-at-large are $17 per year.

To become an AAUW branch student affiliate, join at the local level. Visit www.aauw.org or contact the AAUW Helpline at helpline@aauw.org or 800/326-AAUW (2289) to locate a branch in your area.

Please allow 4–6 weeks for receipt of your new member packet.

AAUW does not share e-mail addresses with third parties.

☐ Occasionally AAUW's membership list is made available to carefully screened companies and organizations. Check here if you do not want your name included on the list.

Personal Information

Name ______________________________

❑ Mrs. ❑ Miss ❑ Ms. ❑ Mr. ❑ Dr.

Street ______________________________

City__________________ State ______ ZIP __________

Phone (H) (______) ______________________

(W) (______) ______________________

Fax (______) ______________________

E-mail address ______________________

College/university ______________________

State ______________________

Degree earned/sought ______________________

Year graduated/anticipated graduation ______________

Gender ❑ Female ❑ Male

I wish to join as an

❑ AAUW Member-at-Large ($49) M08MWTGA11

❑ AAUW Student Affiliate ($17) M08MWTGA11

Total Enclosed $____________

Payment Information

❑ Check or money order payable to AAUW

❑ Credit card

❑ VISA ❑ MasterCard

Card #__ __ __ __ - __ __ __ __ - __ __ __ __ - __ __ __ __

Expiration date ______________________

Name on card ______________________

Signature ______________________

Today's date ______________________

Credit card billing address ❑ Same as above

Name ______________________

Street ______________________

City__________________ State ______ ZIP __________

Mail completed membership application to

AAUW
P.O. Box 96974
Washington, DC 20077-7022

We Need Your Help …

Please give today!

Founded in 1881, the American Association of University Women has championed the rights of women and girls in education and the workplace for more than 125 years. Hundreds of thousands of women and men have contributed their time and financial resources to help provide educational opportunities for women and girls through the AAUW Educational Foundation, which advances gender equity in education and the workplace through fellowships, research, and advocacy.

Today, our message remains as true as ever: Educating women and girls helps individuals, their families, and society. With nearly 100,000 members, 1,300 branches, and 500 college and university partners, AAUW provides a powerful voice for women and girls—in Washington, D.C., our state capitals, and our communities.

AAUW's work would not be possible without generous contributions from people who share its commitment to education, passion for equity, and unwavering belief that women are an instrumental part of leadership, change, and growth. With your support, the Educational Foundation can continue its research and scholarship on issues of importance to women and girls.

❑ **Yes! I** want to contribute to educational and economic opportunities for women and girls.

Please accept my contribution of ❑ $250 ❑ $100 ❑ $50 ❑ $35 ❑ Other (specify______)

Name ______________________________

Address ______________________________

City______________________ State__________ ZIP__________

Daytime telephone ______________________________

E-mail address ______________________________

Payment method

❑ Check or money order payable to the AAUW Educational Foundation

❑ Credit card (check one): ❑ MasterCard ❑ VISA ❑ American Express ❑ Discover

Card no. _ _ _ _ _ _ _ _ _ _ _ _ _ _ _ _

Exp. date ______________________ Today's date ______________________

Name on card ______________________________

Billing address ❑ Same as above

Address ______________________________

City______________________ State__________ ZIP__________

Fax your completed form to 202/463-7169 (credit card payments only) or mail it to

AAUW Development Office, PO Box 630832, Baltimore, MD 21263-0832

To learn more about AAUW or to make contributions on the web, visit www.aauw.org.
The AAUW Educational Foundation is a 501(c)(3) corporation. Gifts are tax-deductible to the extent allowed by law.